YOUR

HOROSCOPE

2019

VIRGO

YOUR PERSONAL HOROSCOPE 2019

VIRGO

24th August–23rd September

igloobooks

Published in 2018
by Igloo Books Ltd
Cottage Farm
Sywell
NN6 0BJ
www.igloobooks.com

Produced for Igloo Books by Foulsham Publishing Ltd, The Old Barrel Store,
Drayman's Lane, Marlow, Bucks SL7 2FF, England

FIR003 0718
2 4 6 8 10 9 7 5 3 1
ISBN: 978-1-78810-565-1

This is an abridged version of material originally published
in Old Moore's Horoscope and Astral Diary.

Cover designed by Nicholas Gage
Edited by Bobby Newlyn-Jones

Printed and manufactured in China

CONTENTS

INTRODUCTION

Your personal horoscopes have been specifically created to allow you to get the most from astrological patterns and the way they have a bearing on not only your zodiac sign, but nuances within it. Using the diary section of the book you can read about the influences and possibilities of each and every day of the year. It will be possible for you to see when you are likely to be cheerful and happy or those times when your nature is in retreat and you will be more circumspect. The diary will help to give you a feel for the specific 'cycles' of astrology and the way they can subtly change your day-to-day life. For example, when you see the sign ☿, this means that the planet Mercury is retrograde at that time. Retrograde means it appears to be running backwards through the zodiac. Such a happening has a significant effect on communication skills, but this is only one small aspect of how the personal horoscope can help you.

With your personal horoscope the story doesn't end with the diary pages. It includes simple ways for you to work out the zodiac sign the Moon occupied at the time of your birth, and what this means for your personality. In addition, if you know the time of day you were born, it is possible to discover your Ascendant, yet another important guide to your personal make-up and potential.

Many readers are interested in relationships and in knowing how well they get on with people of other astrological signs. You might also be interested in the way you appear to very different sorts of individuals. If you are such a person, the section on Venus will be of particular interest. Despite the rapidly changing position of this planet, you can work out your Venus sign, and learn what bearing it will have on your life.

Using your personal horoscope you can travel on one of the most fascinating and rewarding journeys that anyone can take – the journey to a better realisation of self.

THE ESSENCE OF VIRGO

Exploring the Personality of Virgo the Virgin

(24TH AUGUST – 23RD SEPTEMBER)

What's in a sign?

Virgo people tend to be a rather extraordinary sort of mixture. Your ruling planet is Mercury, which makes you inclined to be rather chatty and quite sociable. On the other hand, yours is known as an Earth-ruled zodiac sign, which is usually steady and sometimes quite reserved. Thus, from the start, there are opposing energies ruling your life. This is not a problem when the right sort of balance is achieved and that is what you are looking for all the time. Repressed social and personal communication can make you worrisome, which in turn leads to a slightly fussy tendency that is not your most endearing quality.

At best you are quite ingenious and can usually rely on your strong intuition when weighing up the pros and cons of any given situation. Like all Earth signs you are able to accrue wealth, and work hard to achieve your ultimate objectives in life. However, one is left with the impression that problems arise for Virgo when acquisition takes over. In other words you need to relax more and to enjoy the fruits of your successes on a more regular basis.

Tidiness is important to you, and not just around your home. You particularly don't like loose ends and can be meticulous in your sense of detail. It seems likely that the fictional Sherlock Holmes was a Virgo subject and his ability to get to the absolute root of all situations is a stock-in-trade for the sign of the Virgin. Flexibility is especially important in relationships and you shouldn't become so obsessed with the way surroundings look that you fail to make the most of social opportunities.

Another tendency for Virgo is a need to 'keep up with the Joneses'. Why do you do this? Mainly because like your fellow Mercury-ruled sign of Gemini you haven't really as much confidence

9

as seems to be the case. As a result you want to know that you are as good as anyone else, and if possible better. This can, on occasion, lead to a sort of subconscious race that you can never hope to win. Learn to relax, and to recognise when you are on top anyway, and you are really motoring.

Virgo resources

Virgoan people are not at all short of savvy, and one of the most important considerations about your make-up is that you usually know how to proceed in a practical sense. At your disposal you have an armoury of weapons that can lead to a successful sort of life, especially in a practical and financial sense.

Your ruling planet, Mercury, makes you a good communicator and shows you the way to get on-side with the world at large. This quality means that you are rarely short of the right sort of information that is necessary in order to get things right first time. Where this doesn't prove to be possible you have Earth-sign tenacity, and an ability to work extremely hard for long hours in order to achieve your intended objectives. On the way you tend on the whole to make friends, though you might find it hard to get through life without picking up one or two adversaries too.

Virgo people are capable of being gregarious and gossipy, whilst at the same time retaining an internal discipline, which more perceptive people are inclined to recognise instinctively. You cement secure friendships and that means nearly always having someone to rely on in times of difficulty. But this isn't a one-way street, because you are a very supportive type yourself and would fight tenaciously on behalf of a person or a cause that you supported wholeheartedly. At such times you can appear to be quite brave, even though you could be quaking inside.

A tendency towards being nervy is not always as evident as you might think, mainly because you have the power and ability to keep it behind closed doors. Retaining the secrets of friends, despite your tendency to indulge in gossip, is an important part of your character and is the reason that others learn to trust you. Organisational skills are good and you love to sort out the puzzles of life, which makes you ideal for tedious jobs that many other people would find impossible to complete. Your curiosity knows no bounds and you would go to almost any length to answer questions that are uppermost in your mind at any point in time.

Beneath the surface

So what are you really like? Well, in the case of Virgo this might be the most interesting journey of all, and one that could deeply surprise even some of those people who think they know you very well indeed. First of all it must be remembered that your ruling planet is Mercury, known as the lord of communication. As a result it's important for you to keep in touch with the world at large. That's fine, except for the fact that your Earth-sign tendencies are inclined to make you basically quiet by nature.

Here we find something of a contradiction and one that leads to more than a few misunderstandings. You are particularly sensitive to little changes out there in the cosmos and so can be much more voluble on some days than on others. The result can be that others see you as being somewhat moody, which isn't really the case at all. You are inclined to be fairly nervy and would rarely be quite as confident as you give the impression of being. Although usually robust in terms of general health, this doesn't always seem to be the case and a tendency towards a slightly hypochondriac nature can be the result. Some Virgoans can make an art form out of believing that they are unwell and you need to understand that part of the reason for this lies in your desire for attention.

Another accusation that is levelled at Virgoans is that they are inclined to be fussy over details. This is also an expression of your lack of basic confidence in yourself. For some reason you subconsciously assume that if every last matter is dealt with absolutely, all will work out well. In reality the more relaxed you remain, the better you find your ability to cope with everyday life.

The simple truth is that you are much more capable than your inner nature tends to believe and could easily think more of yourself than you do. You have a logical mind, but also gain from the intuition that is possessed by all Mercury-ruled individuals. The more instinctive you become, the less you worry about things and the more relaxed life can seem to be. You also need to override a natural suspicion of those around you. Trust is a hard thing for you, but a very important one.

Making the best of yourself

There are many ways in which you can exploit the best potentials of your zodiac sign, and at the same time play down some of the less favourable possibilities. From the very start it's important to realise that the main criticism that comes your way from the outside world is that you are too fussy by half. So, simply avoid being critical of others and the way they do things. By all means stick to your own opinions, but avoid forcing them onto other people. If you can get over this hurdle, your personal popularity will already be that much greater. If people love you, you care for them in return – it's as simple as that, because at heart you aren't really very complicated.

Despite the fact that a little humility would go a long way, you also do need to remain sure of yourself. There's no real problem in allowing others their head, while following your own opinions all the same. Use your practical skills to the full and don't rush things just because other people seem to do so. Although you are ruled by quick Mercury you also come from an Earth sign, which means steady progress.

Find outlets to desensitise your over-nervy nature. You can do this with plenty of healthy exercise and by taking an interest in subject matter that isn't of any great importance, but which you find appealing all the same. Avoid concentrating too much on any one thing, because that is the road to paranoia.

Realise that you have an innate sense of what is right, and that if it is utilised in the right way you can make gains for yourself and for the people you love. You have a good fund of ideas, so don't be afraid to use them. Most important of all you need to remain confident but flexible. That's the path to popularity – something you need much more than you might realise.

The impressions you give

This can be something of a problem area to at least some people born under the zodiac sign of Virgo. There isn't much doubt that your heart is in the right place and this fact isn't lost on many observers. All the same, you can appear to be very definite in your opinions, in fact to the point of stubbornness, and you won't give ground when you know you are in the right. A slight problem here might be that Virgoans nearly always think they have the moral and legal high ground. In the majority of cases this may indeed be true, but there are ways and means of putting the message across.

What Virgo needs more than anything else is tact. A combination of Mercury, ruling your means of communication, and your Earth-sign heritage can, on occasions, make you appear to be rather blunt. Mercury also aids in quick thinking and problem solving. The sum total can make it appear that you don't take other people's opinions into account and that you are prepared to railroad your ideas through if necessary.

Most people recognise that you are very capable, and may therefore automatically turn to you for leadership. It isn't certain how you will react under any given circumstance because although you can criticise others, your Earth-sign proclivities don't make you a natural leader. In a strong supportive role you can be wonderful and it is towards this scenario that you might choose to look.

Avoid people accusing you of being fussy by deliberately cultivating flexibility in your thinking and your actions. You are one of the kindest and most capable people to be found anywhere in the zodiac. All you need to do to complete the picture is to let the world at large know what you are. With your natural kindness and your ability to get things done you can show yourself to be a really attractive individual. Look towards a brush-up of your public persona. Deep inside you are organised and caring, though a little nervy. Let people know exactly what you are – it only makes you more human.

The way forward

Before anyone can move forward into anything it is important for them to realise exactly where they are now. In your case this is especially true. Probably the most problematic area of Virgo is in realising not what is being done but rather why. It is the inability to ask this question on a regular basis that leads Virgo into a rut now and again. Habit isn't simply a word to many people born under the zodiac sign of Virgo, it's a religion. The strange thing about this fact is that if you find yourself catapulted, against your will, into a different sort of routine, you soon learn to adopt it as if it were second nature. In other words this way of behaving is endemic, but not necessarily inevitable. The way out of it is simple and comes thanks to your ruling planet of Mercury. Keep talking, and at the same time listen. Adapt your life on a regular basis and say 'So many habits are not necessary' at least ten times a day.

All the same it wouldn't be very prudent to throw out the baby with the bath water. Your ability to stick at things is justifiably legendary. This generally means that you arrive at your desired destination in life, even though it might take you a long time to get there. The usual result is respect from people who don't have your persistence or tenacity.

With regard to love and affection you are in a good position to place a protecting blanket around those you love the most. This is fine, as long as you check regularly that you are not suffocating them with it. If you allow a certain degree of freedom people will respect your concern all the more, and they won't fight against it. By all means communicate your affection and don't allow your natural Earth-sign reserve to get in the way of expressing feelings that are quite definite internally. This is another aspect of letting the world know what you are really like and is of crucial importance to your zodiac sign.

You need variety, and if possible an absence of worry. Only when things are going wrong do Virgoans become the fussy individuals that sometimes attract a little criticism. As long as you feel that you are in charge of your own destiny, you can remain optimistic – another vital requisite for Virgo. With just a little effort you can be one of the most popular and loved people around. Add to this your natural ability to succeed and the prognosis for the sign of the Virgin is very good.

VIRGO ON THE CUSP

Astrological profiles are altered for those people born at either the beginning or the end of a zodiac sign, or, more properly, on the cusps of a sign. In the case of Virgo this would be on the 24th of August and for two or three days after, and similarly at the end of the sign, probably from the 21st to the 23rd of September.

The Leo Cusp – 24th August to 26th August

If anything is designed to lighten the load of being a Virgoan, it's having a Leo quality in the nature too. All Virgoans are inclined to take themselves too seriously on occasions and they don't have half as much self-esteem as they could really use effectively. Being born on the Leo cusp gives better self-confidence, less of the supreme depths which Virgo alone can display and a much more superficial view of many aspects of life. The material success for which Virgo is famous probably won't be lacking, but there will also be a determination to have fun and let the bright, aspiring qualities that are so popular in the Leo character show.

In matters of love, you are likely to be easy-going, bright, bubbly and always willing to have a laugh. You relish good company, and though you sometimes go at things like a bull at a gate, your intentions are true and you know how to get others to like you a great deal. Family matters are right up your street, because not only do you have the ability to put down firm and enduring roots, but you are the most staunch and loyal protector of family values that anyone could wish for.

When it comes to working, you seem to have the best combination of all. You have the ability to work long and hard, achieving your objectives as all Virgoans do, but managing to do so with a smile permanently fixed to your face. You are naturally likely to find yourself at the head of things, where your combination of skills is going to be of the greatest use. This sign combination is to be found in every nook and cranny of the working world but perhaps less frequently in jobs which involve getting your hands dirty.

There are times when you definitely live on your nerves and when you don't get the genuine relaxation that the Virgoan qualities within you demand. Chances are you are much more robust than you consider yourself to be, and as long as you keep busy most of the time you tend to enjoy a contented life. The balance usually works well, because Leo lifts Virgo, whilst Virgo stabilises an often too superficial Lion.

The Libra Cusp – 21st September to 23rd September

Virgo responds well to input from other parts of the zodiac and probably never more so than in the case of the Libran cusp. The reasons for this are very simple: what Virgo on its own lacks, Libra possesses, and it's the same on the other side of the coin. Libra is often flighty and doesn't take enough time to rest, but it is compensated by the balance inherent in the sign, so it weighs things carefully. Virgo on the other hand is deep and sometimes dark, but because it's ruled by capricious little Mercury, it can also be rather too impetuous. The potential break-even point is obvious and usually leads to a fairly easy-going individual, who is intellectual, thoughtful and practical when necessary.

You are a great person to have around in good times and bad, and you know how to have fun. A staunch support and helper to your friends, you enjoy a high degree of popularity, which usually extends to affairs of the heart. There may be more than one of these in your life and it's best for people born on this cusp not to marry in haste or too early in life. But even if you get things wrong first time around, you have the ability to bounce back quickly and don't become easily discouraged. It is good for you to be often in the company of gregarious and interesting people, but you are quite capable of surviving on your own when you have to.

Health matters may be on your mind more than is strictly necessary, and it's true that you can sometimes worry yourself into minor ailments that would not otherwise have existed. It is important for you to get plenty of rest and also to enjoy yourself. The more you work on behalf of others, the less time you spend thinking about your own possible ailments. Anxiety needs to be avoided, often by getting to the root of a problem and solving it quickly.

A capable and committed worker, you are at your best when able to share the decisions, but you are quite reliable when you have to make up your mind alone. You would never bully those beneath you. You are never short of support and you bring joy to life most of the time.

VIRGO AND ITS ASCENDANTS

The nature of every individual on the planet is composed of the rich variety of zodiac signs and planetary positions that were present at the time of their birth. Your Sun sign, which in your case is Virgo, is one of the many factors when it comes to assessing the unique person you are. Probably the most important consideration, other than your Sun sign, is to establish the zodiac sign that was rising over the eastern horizon at the time that you were born. This is your Ascending or Rising sign. Most popular astrology fails to take account of the Ascendant, and yet its importance remains with you from the very moment of your birth, through every day of your life. The Ascendant is evident in the way you approach the world, and so, when meeting a person for the first time, it is this astrological influence that you are most likely to notice first. Our Ascending sign essentially represents what we appear to be, while the Sun sign is what we feel inside ourselves.

The Ascendant also has the potential for modifying our overall nature. For example, if you were born at a time of day when Virgo was passing over the eastern horizon (this would be around the time of dawn) then you would be classed as a double Virgo. As such, you would typify this zodiac sign, both internally and in your dealings with others. However, if your Ascendant sign turned out to be a Fire sign, such as Aries, there would be a profound alteration of nature, away from the expected qualities of Virgo.

One of the reasons why popular astrology often ignores the Ascendant is that it has always been rather difficult to establish. We have found a way to make this possible by devising an easy-to-use table, which you will find on page 157 of this book. Using this, you can establish your Ascendant sign at a glance. You will need to know your rough time of birth, then it is simply a case of following the instructions.

For those readers who have no idea of their time of birth it might be worth allowing a good friend, or perhaps your partner, to read through the section that follows this introduction. Someone who deals with you on a regular basis may easily discover your Ascending sign, even though you could have some difficulty establishing it for yourself. A good understanding of this component of your nature is essential if you want to be aware of that 'other person' who is responsible for the way you make contact with the world at large. Your Sun sign, Ascendant sign, and the other pointers in this book

17

will, together, allow you a far better understanding of what makes you tick as an individual. Peeling back the different layers of your astrological make-up can be an enlightening experience, and the Ascendant may represent one of the most important layers of all.

Virgo with Virgo Ascendant

You get the best of both worlds, and on rare occasions the worst too. Frighteningly efficient, you have the ability to scare people with your constant knack of getting it right. This won't endear you to everyone, particularly those who pride themselves on being disorganised. You make a loyal friend and would do almost anything for someone who is important to you, though you do so in a quiet way because you are not the most noisy of types. Chances are that you possess the ability to write well and you also have a cultured means of verbal communication on those occasions when you really choose to speak out.

It isn't difficult for you to argue your case, though much of the time you refuse to do so and can lock yourself into your own private world for days on end. If you are at ease with yourself you possess a powerful personality, which you can express well. Conversely, you can live on your nerves and cause problems for yourself. Meditation is good, fussing over details that really don't matter at all is less useful. Once you have chosen a particular course of action there are few people around with sufficient will-power to prevent you from getting what you want. Wide open spaces where the hand of nature is all around can make you feel very relaxed.

Virgo with Libra Ascendant

Libra has the ability to lighten almost any load and it is particularly good at doing so when it is brought together with the much more repressed sign of Virgo. To the world at large you seem relaxed, happy and able to cope with most of the pressures that life places upon you. Not only do you deal with your own life in a bright and breezy manner, but you are usually on hand to help others out of any dilemma that they might make for themselves. With excellent powers of communication you leave the world at large in no doubt whatsoever concerning both your opinions and your wishes. It is in the talking stakes that you really excel because Virgo brings the silver tongue of Mercury and Libra adds the Air-sign desire to be in constant touch with the world outside your door.

You like to have a good time and are often found in the company of interesting and stimulating people, who have the ability to bring out the very best in your bright and sparkling personality. Underneath however, there is still much of the worrying Virgoan to be found and this means that you have to learn to relax inside as well as appearing to do so externally. In fact you are much more complex than most people would realise and definitely would not be suited to a life that allowed you too much time to think about yourself.

Virgo with Scorpio Ascendant

This is intensity carried through to the absolute. If you have a problem it is that you fail to externalise all that is going on inside that deep, bubbling cauldron of your inner self. Realising what you are capable of is not a problem, these only start when you have to make it plain to those around you what you want. Part of the reason for this is that you don't always understand yourself. You love intensely and would do absolutely anything for a person you are fond of, even though you might have to inconvenience yourself a great deal on the way. Relationships can cause you slight problems however, since you need to associate with people who at least come somewhere near to understanding what makes you tick. If you manage to bridge the gap between yourself and the world that constantly knocks on your door, you show yourself to be powerful, magnetic and compulsive.

There are times when you definitely prefer to stay quiet though you do have a powerful ability to get your message across when you think it is necessary to do so. There are people around who might think that you are a push-over, but they could easily get a shock when you sense that the time is right to answer back. You probably have a very orderly house and don't care for clutter of any sort.

Virgo with Sagittarius Ascendant

This is a combination that might look rather odd at first sight because these two signs have so very little in common. However the saying goes that opposites attract and in terms of the personality you display to the world this is especially true in your case. Not everyone understands what makes you tick, but you try to show the least complicated face to the world that you can manage to display. You can be deep and secretive on occasions, and yet at other times you can start talking as soon as you climb out of bed and never stop until you are back there again. Inspirational and spontaneous, you take the world by storm on those occasions when you are free from worries and firing on all cylinders. It is a fact that you support your friends, though there are rather more of them than would be the case for Virgo taken on its own and you don't always choose them as wisely as you might.

There are times when you display a temper and although Sagittarius is incapable of bearing a grudge, the same cannot be said for Virgo, which has a better memory than the elephant. For the best results in life you need to relax as much as possible and avoid overheating that powerful and busy brain. Virgo gives you the ability to concentrate on one thing at once, a skill that should be encouraged.

Virgo with Capricorn Ascendant

Your endurance, persistence and concentration are legendary and there is virtually nothing that eludes you once you have the bit between your teeth. You are not the pushy, fussy, go-getting sort of Virgoan but are steady, methodical and very careful. Once you have made up your mind, a whole team of wild horses could not change it and although this can be a distinct blessing at times, it is a quality that can bring odd problems into your life too. The difficulty starts when you adopt a lost or less than sensible cause. Even in the face of overwhelming evidence that you are wrong there is something inside you that prevents any sort of U-turn and so you walk forward as solidly as only you are able, to a destination that won't suit you at all.

There are few people around who are more loyal and constant than you. There is a lighter and brighter side to your nature and the one or two people who are most important in your life will know how to bring it out. You have a wicked sense of humour, particularly if you have had a drink or when you are feeling on top form. Travel does you the world of good, even if there is a part of you that would rather stay at home. You have a potent, powerful and magnetic personality, but for much of the time it is kept carefully hidden.

Virgo with Aquarius Ascendant

How could anyone make convention unconventional? Well, if anyone can manage, you can. There are great contradictions here because on the one hand you always want to do what is expected, but the Aquarian quality within your nature loves to surprise everyone on the way. If you don't always know what you are thinking or doing, it's a pretty safe bet that others won't either, so it's important on occasions to stop and really think. However this is not a pressing concern because you tend to live a fairly happy life and muddle through no matter what. Other people tend to take to you well and it is likely that you will have many friends. You tend to be bright and cheerful and can approach even difficult tasks with the certainty that you have the skills necessary to see them through to their conclusion. Give and take are important factors in the life of any individual and particularly so in your case. Because you can stretch yourself in order to understand what makes other people think and act in the way that they do, you have the reputation of being a good friend and a reliable colleague.

In love you can be somewhat more fickle than the typical Virgoan and yet you are always interesting to live with. Wherever you are, things happen, and you mix a sparkling wit with deep insights.

Virgo with Pisces Ascendant

You might have been accused on occasions of being too sensitive for your own good, a charge that is not entirely without foundation. Certainly you are very understanding of the needs of others, sometimes to the extent that you put everything aside to help them. This would also be true in the case of charities, for you care very much about the world and the people who cling tenaciously to its surface. Your ability to love on a one-to-one basis knows no bounds though you may not discriminate as much as you could, particularly when young, and might have one or two false starts in the love stakes. You don't always choose to verbalise your thoughts and this can cause problems, because there is always so much going on in your mind and Virgo especially needs good powers of communication. Pisces is quieter and you need to force yourself to say what you think when the explanation is important.

You would never betray a confidence and sometimes take on rather more for the sake of your friends than is strictly good for you. This is not a fault, but can cause you problems all the same. Because you are so intuitive there is little that escapes your attention, though you should avoid being pessimistic about your insights. Changes of scenery suit you and extensive travel would bring out the best in what can be a repressed nature at times.

Virgo with Aries Ascendant

Virgo is steady and sure, though also fussy and stubborn. Aries is fast and determined, restless and active. It can be seen already that this is a rather strange meeting of characteristics and because Virgo is ruled by capricious Mercury, the result will change from hour to hour and day to day. It isn't merely that others find it difficult to know where they are with you; they can't even understand what makes you tick. This will make you the subject of endless fascination and attention, at which you will be apparently surprised, but inwardly pleased. If anyone ever really gets to know what goes on in that busy mind they may find the implications very difficult to deal with and it is a fact that only you would have the ability to live inside your head.

As a partner and a parent you are second to none, though you would tend to get on better with your children once they started to grow, since by this time you may be slightly less restricting to their own desires, which will often clash with your own on their behalf. You are capable of give and take and could certainly not be considered selfish, though your desire to get the best from everyone might be misconstrued on occasion.

Virgo with Taurus Ascendant

This combination tends to amplify the Taurean qualities that you naturally possess and this is the case because both Taurus and Virgo are Earth signs. However, there are certain factors related to Virgo that show themselves very differently than the sign's cousin, Taurus. Virgo is more fussy, nervy and pedantic than Taurus and all of these qualities are going to show up in your nature at one level or another. On the plus side you might be slightly less concerned about having a perfect home and a perfect family, and your interest in life appears at a more direct level than that of the true Taurean. You care very much about your home and family and are very loyal to your friends. It's true that you sometimes tend to try and take them over and you can also show a marked tendency to dominate, but your heart is in the right place and people recognise that your caring is genuine.

One problem is that there are very few shades of grey in your life, which is certainly not the case for other zodiac sign combinations. Living your life in the way that you do, there isn't much room for compromise and this fact alone can prove to be something of a problem where relationships are concerned. In a personal sense you need a partner who is willing to be organised and one who relies on your judgements, which don't change all that often.

Virgo with Gemini Ascendant

A Gemini Ascendant means that you are ruled by Mercury, both through your Sun sign and through the sign that was rising at the time of your birth. This means that words are your basic tools in life and you use them to the full. Some writers have this combination, because even speaking to people virtually all the time is not enough. Although you have many friends you are fairly high-minded, which means that you can make enemies too. The fact is that people either care very much for you, or else they don't like you at all. This can be difficult for you to come to terms with because you don't really set out to cause friction – it simply attracts itself to you.

Although you love travel, home is important, too, and there is a basic insecurity in your nature that comes about as a result of an overdose of Mercury, which makes you nervy and sometimes far less confident than anyone would guess. Success in your life may be slower arriving with this combination because you are determined to achieve your objectives on your own terms and this can take time. Always a contradiction, often a puzzle to others, your ultimate happiness in life is directly proportional to the effort you put in, though this should not mean wearing yourself out on the way.

Virgo with Cancer Ascendant

What can this union of zodiac signs bring to the party that isn't there in either Virgo or Cancer alone? Well quite a bit actually. Virgo can be very fussy on occasions and too careful for its own good. The presence of steady, serene Cancer alters the perspectives and allows a smoother, more flowing Virgoan to greet the world. You are chatty, easy to know and exhibit a combination of the practical skills of Virgo, together with the deep and penetrating insights that are typical of Cancer. This can make you appear to be very powerful, and your insights are second to none. You are a born organiser and love to be where things are happening, even if you are only there to help make the sandwiches or to pour the tea. Invariably your role will be much greater but you don't seek personal acclaim and are a good team player on most occasions.

There is a quiet side to your nature and those who live with you will eventually get used to your need for solitude. This seems strange because Virgo is generally such a chatterbox and, taken on its own, is rarely quiet for long. In love you show great affection and a sense of responsibility that makes you an ideal parent, though it is possible sometimes that you care rather more than you are willing to show.

Virgo with Leo Ascendant

Here we have cheerfulness allied to efficiency, which can be a very positive combination most of the time. With all the sense of honour, justice and bravery of the Leo subject, Virgo adds staying power through tedious situations and offers you a slightly more serious view of life than we would expect from the Lion alone. In almost any situation you can keep going until you get to your chosen destination and you also find the time to reach out to the people who need your unique nature the most. Few would deny your kindness, though you can attract a little envy because it seems as though yours is the sort of personality that everyone else wants.

Most people born with this combination have a radiant smile and will do their best to think situations through carefully. If there is a tendency to be foolhardy, it is carefully masked beneath a covering of Virgoan common sense. Family matters are dealt with efficiently and with great love. Some might see you as close one moment and distant the next. The truth is that you are always on the go and have a thousand different things to think about, all at the same time. On the whole your presence is noticed and you may represent the most loyal friend of them all.

Virgo with Leo Ascendant

THE MOON AND THE PART IT PLAYS IN YOUR LIFE

In astrology the Moon is probably the single most important heavenly body after the Sun. Its unique position, as partner to the Earth on its journey around the solar system, means that the Moon appears to pass through the signs of the zodiac extremely quickly. The zodiac position of the Moon at the time of your birth plays a great part in personal character and is especially significant in the build-up of your emotional nature.

Your Own Moon Sign

Discovering the position of the Moon at the time of your birth has always been notoriously difficult because tracking the complex zodiac positions of the Moon is not easy. This process has been reduced to three simple stages with our Lunar Tables. A breakdown of the Moon's zodiac positions can be found from page 35 onwards, so that once you know what your Moon Sign is, you can see what part this plays in the overall build-up of your personal character.

If you follow the instructions on the next page you will soon be able to work out exactly what zodiac sign the Moon occupied on the day that you were born and you can then go on to compare the reading for this position with those of your Sun sign and your Ascendant. It is partly the comparison between these three important positions that goes towards making you the unique individual you are.

How To Discover Your Moon Sign

This is a three-stage process. You may need a pen and a piece of paper but if you follow the instructions below the process should only take a minute or so.

STAGE 1 First of all you need to know the Moon Age at the time of your birth. If you look at Moon Table 1, on page 33, you will find all the years between 1921 and 2019 down the left side. Find the year of your birth and then trace across to the right to the month of your birth. Where the two intersect you will find a number. This is the date of the New Moon in the month that you were born. You now need to count forward the number of days between the New Moon and your own birthday. For example, if the New Moon in the month of your birth was shown as being the 6th and you were born on the 20th, your Moon Age Day would be 14. If the New Moon in the month of your birth came after your birthday, you need to count forward from the New Moon in the previous month. Whatever the result, jot this number down so that you do not forget it.

STAGE 2 Take a look at Moon Table 2 on page 34. Down the left hand column look for the date of your birth. Now trace across to the month of your birth. Where the two meet you will find a letter. Copy this letter down alongside your Moon Age Day.

STAGE 3 Moon Table 3 on page 34 will supply you with the zodiac sign the Moon occupied on the day of your birth. Look for your Moon Age Day down the left hand column and then for the letter you found in Stage 2. Where the two converge you will find a zodiac sign and this is the sign occupied by the Moon on the day that you were born.

Your Zodiac Moon Sign Explained

You will find a profile of all zodiac Moon Signs on pages 35 to 38, showing in yet another way how astrology helps to make you into the individual that you are. In each daily entry of the Astral Diary you can find the zodiac position of the Moon for every day of the year. This also allows you to discover your lunar birthdays. Since the Moon passes through all the signs of the zodiac in about a month, you can expect something like twelve lunar birthdays each year. At these times you are likely to be emotionally steady and able to make the sort of decisions that have real, lasting value.

MOON TABLE 1

YEAR	JUL	AUG	SEP	YEAR	JUL	AUG	SEP	YEAR	JUL	AUG	SEP
1921	5	3	2	1954	29	28	27	1987	25	24	23
1922	24	22	21	1955	19	17	16	1988	13	12	11
1923	14	12	10	1956	8	6	4	1989	3	1/31	29
1924	2/31	30	28	1957	27	25	23	1990	22	20	19
1925	20	19	18	1958	16	15	13	1991	11	9	8
1926	9	8	7	1959	6	4	3	1992	29	28	26
1927	28	27	25	1960	24	22	21	1993	19	17	16
1928	17	16	14	1961	12	11	10	1994	8	7	5
1929	6	5	3	1962	1/31	30	28	1995	27	26	24
1930	25	24	22	1963	20	19	17	1996	15	14	13
1931	15	13	12	1964	9	7	6	1997	4	3	2
1932	3	2/31	30	1965	28	26	25	1998	23	22	20
1933	22	21	19	1966	17	16	14	1999	13	11	10
1934	11	10	9	1967	7	5	4	2000	1/31	29	27
1935	30	29	27	1968	25	24	23	2001	20	19	17
1936	18	17	15	1969	13	12	11	2002	9	8	6
1937	8	6	4	1970	4	2	1	2003	28	27	26
1938	27	25	23	1971	22	20	19	2004	16	14	13
1939	16	15	13	1972	11	9	8	2005	6	4	3
1940	5	4	2	1973	29	28	27	2006	25	23	22
1941	24	22	21	1974	19	17	16	2007	15	13	12
1942	13	12	10	1975	9	7	5	2008	31	31	30
1943	2	1/30	29	1976	27	25	23	2009	22	20	19
1944	20	18	17	1977	16	14	13	2010	12	10	8
1945	9	8	6	1978	5	4	2	2011	2/31	29	27
1946	28	26	25	1979	24	22	21	2012	19	17	16
1947	17	16	14	1980	12	11	10	2013	7	6	4
1948	6	5	3	1981	1/31	29	28	2014	25	24	23
1949	25	24	23	1982	20	19	17	2015	16	15	13
1950	15	13	12	1983	10	8	7	2016	4	2	1
1951	4	2	1	1984	28	26	25	2017	23	22	20
1952	23	20	19	1985	17	16	14	2018	13	11	9
1953	11	9	8	1986	7	5	4	2019	2/31	30	28

TABLE 2

DAY	AUG	SEP
1	U	X
2	U	X
3	V	X
4	V	Y
5	V	Y
6	V	Y
7	V	Y
8	V	Y
9	V	Y
10	V	Y
11	V	Y
12	V	Y
13	V	Y
14	W	Z
15	W	Z
16	W	Z
17	W	Z
18	W	Z
19	W	Z
20	W	Z
21	W	Z
22	W	Z
23	W	Z
24	X	a
25	X	a
26	X	a
27	X	a
28	X	a
29	X	a
30	X	a
31	X	–

MOON TABLE 3

M/D	U	V	W	X	Y	Z	a
0	LE	LE	LE	VI	VI	LI	LI
1	LE	VI	VI	VI	LI	LI	LI
2	VI	VI	VI	LI	LI	LI	LI
3	VI	VI	LI	LI	LI	SC	SC
4	LI	LI	LI	LI	SC	SC	SC
5	LI	LI	SC	SC	SC	SC	SA
6	LI	SC	SC	SC	SA	SA	SA
7	SC	SC	SA	SA	SA	SA	SA
8	SC	SC	SA	SA	SA	CP	CP
9	SA	SA	SA	SA	CP	CP	CP
10	SA	SA	CP	CP	CP	CP	AQ
11	CP	CP	CP	CP	AQ	AQ	AQ
12	CP	CP	AQ	AQ	AQ	AQ	PI
13	CP	CP	AQ	AQ	AQ	PI	PI
14	AQ	AQ	PI	PI	PI	PI	AR
15	AQ	AQ	PI	PI	PI	PI	AR
16	AQ	PI	PI	PI	AR	AR	AR
17	PI	PI	PI	AR	AR	AR	AR
18	PI	PI	AR	AR	AR	AR	TA
19	PI	AR	AR	AR	TA	TA	TA
20	AR	AR	TA	TA	TA	TA	GE
21	AR	TA	TA	TA	GE	GE	GE
22	TA	TA	TA	GE	GE	GE	GE
23	TA	TA	GE	GE	GE	GE	CA
24	TA	GE	GE	GE	CA	CA	CA
25	GE	GE	CA	CA	CA	CA	CA
26	GE	CA	CA	CA	LE	LE	LE
27	CA	CA	CA	LE	LE	LE	LE
28	CA	CA	LE	LE	LE	LE	VI
29	CA	LE	LE	LE	VI	VI	VI

AR = Aries, TA = Taurus, GE = Gemini, CA = Cancer, LE = Leo, VI = Virgo,
LI = Libra, SC = Scorpio, SA = Sagittarius, CP = Capricorn, AQ = Aquarius, PI = Pisces

MOON SIGNS

Moon in Aries

You have a strong imagination, courage, determination and a desire to do things in your own way and forge your own path through life.

Originality is a key attribute; you are seldom stuck for ideas although your mind is changeable and you could take the time to focus on individual tasks. Often quick-tempered, you take orders from few people and live life at a fast pace. Avoid health problems by taking regular time out for rest and relaxation.

Emotionally, it is important that you talk to those you are closest to and work out your true feelings. Once you discover that people are there to help, there is less necessity for you to do everything yourself.

Moon in Taurus

The Moon in Taurus gives you a courteous and friendly manner, which means you are likely to have many friends.

The good things in life mean a lot to you, as Taurus is an Earth sign that delights in experiences which please the senses. Hence you are probably a lover of good food and drink, which may in turn mean you need to keep an eye on the bathroom scales, especially as looking good is also important to you.

Emotionally you are fairly stable and you stick by your own standards. Taureans do not respond well to change. Intuition also plays an important part in your life.

Moon in Gemini

You have a warm-hearted character, sympathetic and eager to help others. At times reserved, you can also be articulate and chatty: this is part of the paradox of Gemini, which always brings duplicity to the nature. You are interested in current affairs, have a good intellect, and are good company and likely to have many friends. Most of your friends have a high opinion of you and would be ready to defend you should the need arise. However, this is usually unnecessary, as you are quite capable of defending yourself in any verbal confrontation.

Travel is important to your inquisitive mind and you find intellectual stimulus in mixing with people from different cultures. You also gain much from reading, writing and the arts but you do need plenty of rest and relaxation in order to avoid fatigue.

Moon in Cancer

The Moon in Cancer at the time of birth is a fortunate position as Cancer is the Moon's natural home. This means that the qualities of compassion and understanding given by the Moon are especially enhanced in your nature, and you are friendly and sociable and cope well with emotional pressures. You cherish home and family life, and happily do the domestic tasks. Your surroundings are important to you and you hate squalor and filth. You are likely to have a love of music and poetry.

Your basic character, although at times changeable like the Moon itself, depends on symmetry. You aim to make your surroundings comfortable and harmonious, for yourself and those close to you.

Moon in Leo

The best qualities of the Moon and Leo come together to make you warm-hearted, fair, ambitious and self-confident. With good organisational abilities, you invariably rise to a position of responsibility in your chosen career. This is fortunate as you don't enjoy being an 'also-ran' and would rather be an important part of a small organisation than a menial in a large one.

You should be lucky in love, and happy, provided you put in the effort to make a comfortable home for yourself and those close to you. It is likely that you will have a love of pleasure, sport, music and literature. Life brings you many rewards, most of them as a direct result of your own efforts, although you may be luckier than average and ready to make the best of any situation.

Moon in Virgo

You are endowed with good mental abilities and a keen receptive memory, but you are never ostentatious or pretentious. Naturally quite reserved, you still have many friends, especially of the opposite sex. Marital relationships must be discussed carefully and worked at so that they remain harmonious, as personal attachments can be a problem if you do not give them your full attention.

Talented and persevering, you possess artistic qualities and are a good homemaker. Earning your honours through genuine merit, you work long and hard towards your objectives but show little pride in your achievements. Many short journeys will be undertaken in your life.

Moon in Libra

With the Moon in Libra you are naturally popular and make friends easily. People like you, probably more than you realise, you bring fun to a party and are a natural diplomat. For all its good points, Libra is not the most stable of astrological signs and, as a result, your emotions can be a little unstable too. Therefore, although the Moon in Libra is said to be good for love and marriage, your Sun sign and Rising sign will have an important effect on your emotional and loving qualities.

You must remember to relate to others in your decision-making. Co-operation is crucial because Libra represents the 'balance' of life that can only be achieved through harmonious relationships. Conformity is not easy for you because Libra likes its independence.

Moon in Scorpio

Some people might call you pushy. In fact, all you really want to do is to live life to the full and protect yourself and your family from the pressures of life. Take care to avoid giving the impression of being sarcastic or impulsive and use your energies wisely and constructively.

You have great courage and you invariably achieve your goals by force of personality and sheer effort. You are fond of mystery and are good at predicting the outcome of situations and events. Travel experiences can be beneficial to you.

You may experience problems if you do not take time to examine your motives in a relationship, and also if you allow jealousy, always a feature of Scorpio, to cloud your judgement.

Moon in Sagittarius

The Moon in Sagittarius helps to make you a generous individual with humanitarian qualities and a kind heart. Restlessness may be intrinsic as your mind is seldom still. Perhaps because of this, you have a need for change that could lead you to several major moves during your adult life. You are not afraid to stand your ground when you know your judgement is right, you speak directly and have good intuition.

At work you are quick, efficient and versatile and so you make an ideal employee. You need work to be intellectually demanding and do not enjoy tedious routines.

In relationships, you anger quickly if faced with stupidity or deception, though you are just as quick to forgive and forget. Emotionally, there are times when your heart rules your head.

Moon in Capricorn

The Moon in Capricorn makes you popular and likely to come into the public eye in some way. The watery Moon is not entirely comfortable in the Earth sign of Capricorn and this may lead to some difficulties in the early years of life. An initial lack of creative ability and indecision must be overcome before the true qualities of patience and perseverance inherent in Capricorn can show through.

You have good administrative ability and are a capable worker, and if you are careful you can accumulate wealth. But you must be cautious and take professional advice in partnerships, as you are open to deception. You may be interested in social or welfare work, which suit your organisational skills and sympathy for others.

Moon in Aquarius

The Moon in Aquarius makes you an active and agreeable person with a friendly, easy-going nature. Sympathetic to the needs of others, you flourish in a laid-back atmosphere. You are broad-minded, fair and open to suggestion, although sometimes you have an unconventional quality which others can find hard to understand.

You are interested in the strange and curious, and in old articles and places. You enjoy trips to these places and gain much from them. Political, scientific and educational work interests you and you might choose a career in science or technology.

Money-wise, you make gains through innovation and concentration and Lunar Aquarians often tackle more than one job at a time. In love you are kind and honest.

Moon in Pisces

You have a kind, sympathetic nature, somewhat retiring at times, but you always take account of others' feelings and help when you can.

Personal relationships may be problematic, but as life goes on you can learn from your experiences and develop a better understanding of yourself and the world around you.

You have a fondness for travel, appreciate beauty and harmony and hate disorder and strife. You may be fond of literature and would make a good writer or speaker yourself. You have a creative imagination and may come across as an incurable romantic. You have strong intuition, maybe bordering on a mediumistic quality, which sets you apart from the mass. You may not be rich in cash terms, but your personal gifts are worth more than gold.

VIRGO IN LOVE

Discover how compatible in love you are with people from the same and other signs of the zodiac. Five stars equals a match made in heaven!

Virgo meets Virgo

Unlike many same-sign combinations this is not a five-star pairing, for one very good reason. Virgo needs to react with other signs to reveal its hidden best side. Two Virgoans together, although enjoying some happiness, will not present a dynamic, sparkling and carefree appearance. They should run an efficient and financially sound household, but that all-important ingredient, passion, may be distinctly low-key. Star rating: ***

Virgo meets Libra

There have been some rare occasions when this match has found great success, but usually the inward-looking Virgoan depresses the naturally gregarious Libran. Libra appears self-confident but is not so beneath the surface and needs encouragement to develop inner confidence, which may not come from Virgo. Constancy can be a problem for Libra, who also tires easily and may find Virgo dull. A less serious approach from Virgo is needed to make this work. Star rating: **

Virgo meets Scorpio

There are one or two potential difficulties here, but there is also a meeting point from which to overcome them. Virgo is very caring and protective, a trait which Scorpio understands and even emulates. Both signs are consistent, but also sarcastic. Scorpio will impress Virgo with its serious side, and may also uncover a hidden passion in Virgo which all too often lies deep within its Earth-sign nature. Material success is very likely, with Virgo taking the lion's share of domestic chores and family responsibilities. Star rating: ***

Virgo meets Sagittarius

There can be some strange happenings in this relationship. Sagittarius and Virgo view life so differently there are always new discoveries. Virgo is much more of a home bird than Sagittarius, but that won't matter if the Archer introduces its hectic social life gradually. More importantly, Sagittarius understands that it takes Virgo a long time to free its hidden 'inner sprite', but once free it will be fun all the way – until Virgo's thrifty nature takes over. There are great possibilities, but effort is required. Star rating: ***

Virgo meets Capricorn

One of the best possible combinations, because Virgo and Capricorn have an instinctive understanding. Both signs know the value of dedicated hard work and apply it equally in a relationship and other areas of life. Two of the most practical signs, nothing is beyond their ken, even if to outsiders they appear rather sterile or lacking in 'oomph'. What matters most is that the individuals are happy, and with so much in common, the likelihood of mutual material success and a shared devotion to home and family, there isn't much doubt of that. Star rating: *****

Virgo meets Aquarius

Aquarius is a strange sign because no matter how well one knows it, it always manages to surprise, and for this reason, against the odds, it's quite likely that Aquarius will form a successful relationship with Virgo. Aquarius is changeable, unpredictable and often quite 'odd' while Virgo is steady, a fuss-pot and very practical. Herein lies the key. What one sign needs, the other provides and that may be the surest recipe for success imaginable. On-lookers may not know why the couple are happy, but they will recognise that this is the case. Star rating: ****

Virgo meets Pisces

This looks an unpromising match from beginning to end. There are exceptions to every rule, particularly where Pisces is concerned, but these two signs are both so deep it's hard to imagine that they could ever find what makes the other tick. Virgo's ruminations are extremely materialistic, while Pisces exists in a world of deep-felt, poorly expressed emotion. Pisces and Virgo might find they don't talk much, so only in a contemplative, almost monastic, match would they ever get on. Still, in a vast zodiac, anything is possible. Star rating: **

Virgo meets Aries

Neither of these signs really understands the other, and that could easily lead to a clash. Virgo is so pedantic, which will drive Aries up the wall, while Aries always wants to be moving on to the next objective before Virgo is even settled with the last one. It will take time for these two to get to know each other, but this is a great business matching. If a personal relationship is seen in these terms then the prognosis can be quite good, but on the whole, this is not an inspiring match. Star rating: ***

Virgo meets Taurus

This is a difficult basis for a successful relationship, and yet it often works. Both signs are from the Earth element, so have a common-sense approach to life. They have a mutual understanding, and share many interests. Taurus understands and copes well with Virgo's fussy nature, while Virgo revels in the Bull's tidy and artistic qualities. Both sides are committed to achieving lasting material success. There won't be fireworks, and the match may lack a certain 'spiritual' feel, but as that works both ways it may not be a problem. Star rating: *****

Virgo meets Gemini

The fact that both these signs are ruled by the planet Mercury might at first seem good but, unfortunately, Mercury works very differently in these signs. Gemini is untidy, flighty, quick, changeable and easily bored, while Virgo is fastidious, steady and constant. If Virgo is willing to accept some anarchy all can be well, but this is not usually the case. Virgoans are deep thinkers and may find Gemini a little superficial. This pair can be compatible intellectually, though even this side isn't without its problems. Star rating: ***

Virgo meets Cancer

This match has little chance of success, for fairly simple reasons: Cancer's generous affection will be submerged by the Virgoan depths, not because Virgo is uncaring, but because it expresses itself so differently. As both signs are naturally quiet, things might become a bit boring. They would be mutually supportive, possibly financially successful and have a very tidy house, but they won't share much sparkle, enthusiasm, risk-taking or passion. If this pair were stranded on a desert island, they might live at different ends. Star rating: **

Virgo meets Leo

There is a chance for this couple, but it won't be trouble-free. Leo and Virgo view life very differently: Virgo is of a serious nature and struggles to relate to Leo's relentless optimism and cheerfulness and can find it annoying. Leo, meanwhile, may find Virgo stodgy, sometimes dark and uninspiring. The saving grace comes through communication – Leo knows how to make Virgo talk, which is what it needs. If this pair find happiness, though, it may be a case of opposites attract! Star rating: ***

VENUS:
THE PLANET OF LOVE

If you look up at the sky around sunset or sunrise you will often see Venus in close attendance to the Sun. It is arguably one of the most beautiful sights of all and there is little wonder that historically it became associated with the goddess of love. But although Venus does play an important part in the way you view love and in the way others see you romantically, this is only one of the spheres of influence that it enjoys in your overall character.

Venus has a part to play in the more cultured side of your life and has much to do with your appreciation of art, literature, music and general creativity. Even the way you look is responsive to the part of the zodiac that Venus occupied at the start of your life, though this fact is also down to your Sun sign and Ascending sign. If, at the time you were born, Venus occupied one of the more gregarious zodiac signs, you will be more likely to wear your heart on your sleeve, as well as to be more attracted to entertainment, social gatherings and good company. If on the other hand Venus occupied a quiet zodiac sign at the time of your birth, you would tend to be more retiring and less willing to shine in public situations.

It's good to know what part the planet Venus plays in your life for it can have a great bearing on the way you appear to the rest of the world and since we all have to mix with others, you can learn to make the very best of what Venus has to offer you.

One of the great complications in the past has always been trying to establish exactly what zodiac position Venus enjoyed when you were born because the planet is notoriously difficult to track. However, we have solved that problem by creating a table that is exclusive to your Sun sign, which you will find on the following page.

Establishing your Venus sign could not be easier. Just look up the year of your birth on the next page and you will see a sign of the Zodiac. This was the sign that Venus occupied in the period covered by your sign in that year. If Venus occupied more than one sign during the period, this is indicated by the date on which the sign changed, and the name of the new sign. For instance, if you were born in 1950, Venus was in Leo until the 10th September, after which time it was in Virgo. If you were born before 10th September your Venus sign is Leo, if you were born on or after 10th September, your Venus sign is Virgo. Once you have established the position of Venus at the time of your birth, you can then look in the pages which follow to see how this has a bearing on your life as a whole.

1921 CANCER / 31.8 LEO
1922 LIBRA / 8.9 SCORPIO
1923 LEO / 28.8 VIRGO /
   20.9 LIBRA
1924 CANCER / 9.9 LEO
1925 LIBRA / 16.9 SCORPIO
1926 LEO / 12.9 VIRGO
1927 VIRGO
1928 VIRGO / 5.9 LIBRA
1929 CANCER / 31.8 LEO
1930 LIBRA / 7.9 SCORPIO
1931 LEO / 28.8 VIRGO /
   20.9 LIBRA
1932 CANCER / 9.9 LEO
1933 LIBRA / 16.9 SCORPIO
1934 LEO / 11.9 VIRGO
1935 VIRGO
1936 VIRGO / 4.9 LIBRA
1937 CANCER / 31.8 LEO
1938 LIBRA / 7.9 SCORPIO
1939 LEO / 27.8 VIRGO /
   19.9 LIBRA
1940 CANCER / 9.9 LEO
1941 LIBRA / 15.9 SCORPIO
1942 LEO / 11.9 VIRGO
1943 VIRGO
1944 VIRGO / 4.9 LIBRA
1945 CANCER / 30.8 LEO
1946 LIBRA / 7.9 SCORPIO
1947 LEO / 27.8 VIRGO /
   18.9 LIBRA
1948 CANCER / 9.9 LEO
1949 LIBRA / 15.9 SCORPIO
1950 LEO / 10.9 VIRGO
1951 VIRGO
1952 VIRGO / 3.9 LIBRA
1953 CANCER / 30.8 LEO
1954 LIBRA / 7.9 SCORPIO
1955 LEO / 26.8 VIRGO /
   17.9 LIBRA
1956 CANCER / 8.9 LEO
1957 LIBRA / 15.9 SCORPIO
1958 LEO / 10.9 VIRGO
1959 VIRGO / 20.9 LEO
1960 VIRGO / 3.9 LIBRA
1961 CANCER / 30.8 LEO
1962 LIBRA / 8.9 SCORPIO
1963 LEO / 26.8 VIRGO /
   17.9 LIBRA
1964 CANCER / 8.9 LEO
1965 LIBRA / 15.9 SCORPIO
1966 LEO / 9.9 VIRGO
1967 VIRGO / 10.9 LEO
1968 VIRGO / 2.9 LIBRA

1969 CANCER / 29.8 LEO
1970 LIBRA / 8.9 SCORPIO
1971 LEO / 25.8 VIRGO /
   16.9 LIBRA
1972 CANCER / 8.9 LEO
1973 LIBRA / 14.9 SCORPIO
1974 LEO / 8.9 VIRGO
1975 VIRGO / 3.9 LEO
1976 VIRGO / 2.9 LIBRA
1977 CANCER / 29.8 LEO
1978 LIBRA / 8.9 SCORPIO
1979 VIRGO / 16.9 LIBRA
1980 CANCER / 8.9 LEO
1981 LIBRA / 14.9 SCORPIO
1982 LEO / 7.9 VIRGO
1983 VIRGO / 28.8 LEO
1984 VIRGO / 2.9 LIBRA
1985 CANCER / 28.8 LEO
1986 LIBRA / 8.9 SCORPIO
1987 VIRGO / 15.9 LIBRA
1988 CANCER / 7.9 LEO
1989 LIBRA / 13.9 SCORPIO
1990 LEO / 7.9 VIRGO
1991 LEO
1992 VIRGO / 1.9 LIBRA
1993 CANCER / 28.8 LEO
1994 LIBRA / 8.9 SCORPIO
1995 VIRGO / 15.9 LIBRA
1996 CANCER / 7.9 LEO
1997 LIBRA / 12.9 SCORPIO
1998 LEO / 6.9 VIRGO
1999 LEO
2000 VIRGO / 1.9 LIBRA
2001 CANCER / 28.8 LEO
2002 LIBRA / 8.9 SCORPIO
2003 VIRGO / 15.9 LIBRA
2004 CANCER / 6.9 LEO
2005 LIBRA / 10.9 SCORPIO
2006 LEO / 4.9 VIRGO
2007 LEO
2008 VIRGO / 1.9 LIBRA
2009 CANCER / 28.8 LEO
2010 LIBRA / 8.9 SCORPIO
2011 VIRGO / 15.9 LIBRA
2012 CANCER / 6.9 LEO
2013 LIBRA / 10.9 SCORPIO
2014 LEO / 4.9 VIRGO
2015 LEO
2016 VIRGO / 31.8 LIBRA
2017 CANCER / 28.8 LEO
2018 LIBRA/ 8.9 SCORPIO
2019 VIRGO/ 15.9 LIBRA

VENUS THROUGH THE ZODIAC SIGNS

Venus in Aries

Amongst other things, the position of Venus in Aries indicates a fondness for travel, music and all creative pursuits. Your nature tends to be affectionate and you would try not to create confusion or difficulty for others if it could be avoided. Many people with this planetary position have a great love of the theatre, and mental stimulation is of the greatest importance. Early romantic attachments are common with Venus in Aries, so it is very important to establish a genuine sense of romantic continuity. Early marriage is not recommended, especially if it is based on sympathy. You may give your heart a little too readily on occasions.

Venus in Taurus

You are capable of very deep feelings and your emotions tend to last for a very long time. This makes you a trusting partner and lover, whose constancy is second to none. In life you are precise and careful and always try to do things the right way. Although this means an ordered life, which you are comfortable with, it can also lead you to be rather too fussy for your own good. Despite your pleasant nature, you are very fixed in your opinions and quite able to speak your mind. Others are attracted to you and historical astrologers always quoted this position of Venus as being very fortunate in terms of marriage. However, if you find yourself involved in a failed relationship, it could take you a long time to trust again.

Venus in Gemini

As with all associations related to Gemini, you tend to be quite versatile, anxious for change and intelligent in your dealings with the world at large. You may gain money from more than one source but you are equally good at spending it. There is an inference here that you are a good communicator, via either the written or the spoken word, and you love to be in the company of interesting people. Always on the look-out for culture, you may also be very fond of music, and love to indulge the curious and cultured side of your nature. In romance you tend to have more than one relationship and could find yourself associated with someone who has previously been a friend or even a distant relative.

Venus in Cancer

You often stay close to home because you are very fond of family and enjoy many of your most treasured moments when you are with those you love. Being naturally sympathetic, you will always do anything you can to support those around you, even people you hardly know at all. This charitable side of your nature is your most noticeable trait and is one of the reasons why others are naturally so fond of you. Being receptive and in some cases even psychic, you can see through to the soul of most of those with whom you come into contact. You may not commence too many romantic attachments but when you do give your heart, it tends to be unconditionally.

Venus in Leo

It must become quickly obvious to almost anyone you meet that you are kind, sympathetic and yet determined enough to stand up for anyone or anything that is truly important to you. Bright and sunny, you warm the world with your natural enthusiasm and would rarely do anything to hurt those around you, or at least not intentionally. In romance you are ardent and sincere, though some may find your style just a little overpowering. Gains come through your contacts with other people and this could be especially true with regard to romance, for love and money often come hand in hand for those who were born with Venus in Leo. People claim to understand you, though you are more complex than you seem.

Venus in Virgo

Your nature could well be fairly quiet no matter what your Sun sign might be, though this fact often manifests itself as an inner peace and would not prevent you from being basically sociable. Some delays and even the odd disappointment in love cannot be ruled out with this planetary position, though it's a fact that you will usually find the happiness you look for in the end. Catapulting yourself into romantic entanglements that you know to be rather ill-advised is not sensible, and it would be better to wait before you committed yourself exclusively to any one person. It is the essence of your nature to serve the world at large and through doing so it is possible that you will attract money at some stage in your life.

Venus in Libra

Venus is very comfortable in Libra and bestows upon those people who have this planetary position a particular sort of kindness that is easy to recognise. This is a very good position for all sorts of friendships and also for romantic attachments that usually bring much joy into your life. Few individuals with Venus in Libra would avoid marriage and since you are capable of great depths of love, it is likely that you will find a contented personal life. You like to mix with people of integrity and intelligence but don't take kindly to scruffy surroundings or work that means getting your hands too dirty. Careful speculation, good business dealings and money through marriage all seem fairly likely.

Venus in Scorpio

You are quite open and tend to spend money quite freely, even on those occasions when you don't have very much. Although your intentions are always good, there are times when you get yourself into the odd scrape and this can be particularly true when it comes to romance, which you may come to late or from a rather unexpected direction. Certainly you have the power to be happy and to make others contented on the way, but you find the odd stumbling block on your journey through life and it could seem that you have to work harder than those around you. As a result of this, you gain a much deeper understanding of the true value of personal happiness than many people ever do, and are likely to achieve true contentment in the end.

Venus in Sagittarius

You are lighthearted, cheerful and always able to see the funny side of any situation. These facts enhance your popularity, which is especially high with members of the opposite sex. You should never have to look too far to find romantic interest in your life, though it is just possible that you might be too willing to commit yourself before you are certain that the person in question is right for you. Part of the problem here extends to other areas of life too. The fact is that you like variety in everything and so can tire of situations that fail to offer it. All the same, if you choose wisely and learn to understand your restless side, then great happiness can be yours.

Venus in Capricorn

The most notable trait that comes from Venus in this position is that it makes you trustworthy and able to take on all sorts of responsibilities in life. People are instinctively fond of you and love you all the more because you are always ready to help those who are in any form of need. Social and business popularity can be yours and there is a magnetic quality to your nature that is particularly attractive in a romantic sense. Anyone who wants a partner for a lover, a spouse and a good friend too would almost certainly look in your direction. Constancy is the hallmark of your nature and unfaithfulness would go right against the grain. You might sometimes be a little too trusting.

Venus in Aquarius

This location of Venus offers a fondness for travel and a desire to try out something new at every possible opportunity. You are extremely easy to get along with and tend to have many friends from varied backgrounds, classes and inclinations. You like to live a distinct sort of life and gain a great deal from moving about, both in a career sense and with regard to your home. It is not out of the question that you could form a romantic attachment to someone who comes from far away or be attracted to a person of a distinctly artistic and original nature. What you cannot stand is jealousy, for you have friends of both sexes and would want to keep things that way.

Venus in Pisces

The first thing people tend to notice about you is your wonderful, warm smile. Being very charitable by nature you will do anything to help others, even if you don't know them well. Much of your life may be spent sorting out situations for other people, but it is very important to feel that you are living for yourself too. In the main, you remain cheerful, and tend to be quite attractive to members of the opposite sex. Where romantic attachments are concerned, you could be drawn to people who are significantly older or younger than yourself or to someone with a unique career or point of view. It might be best for you to avoid marrying whilst you are still very young.

VIRGO:
2018 DIARY PAGES

October

2018

1 MONDAY
Moon Age Day 22   Moon Sign Gemini

The week starts out well and it looks as though this is going to be a good time for broadening your horizons in some way. Take every opportunity to try something new and don't be held back simply because others don't share your point of view. Avoid family arguments by getting out of the house if necessary and giving yourself space to breathe.

2 TUESDAY
Moon Age Day 23   Moon Sign Cancer

You can afford to indulge your ego today and allow others to make a fuss of you. Your accomplishments look good when viewed through the eyes of family members and friends. Of course you know that you are only part of the way towards some chosen destinations but it's good to know people notice your efforts.

3 WEDNESDAY
Moon Age Day 24   Moon Sign Cancer

Whether you are at work or play today you tend to surround yourself with some interesting people and you should be having a generally good time. Your outgoing and happy nature is definitely on display and that means people generally will be doing all they can for you. This ought to be a rewarding interlude.

4 THURSDAY
Moon Age Day 25   Moon Sign Leo

There seems to be so much happening around you at the moment, especially in your love life, that you can become dizzy with the potential. Away from romance you can make new friendships and also rekindle an old flame that may have burned lower recently. Don't be surprised if you are flavour of the month to many people.

5 FRIDAY
Moon Age Day 26   Moon Sign Leo

Now you are more than willing to put in the time and effort to anything you see as being necessary to your own well being and that of those you care for. Once again, you should find that romance is high on your agenda and also that of your partner. If you have just started a new relationship things should be going well.

6 SATURDAY
Moon Age Day 27   Moon Sign Virgo

With the lunar high comes a certainty in your mind that you are going in the right direction generally speaking. Take advantage of every opportunity to make a good impression and be prepared to push your luck as much as you can. There is room for variation in your schedule today, which the position of the Moon supports.

7 SUNDAY
Moon Age Day 28   Moon Sign Virgo

Now filled with optimism and high spirits, you need to make today special in some way. Giving others a helping hand might not be a bad start and you should also be thinking in terms of changes you can make in and around your home. Best of all, you feel the need to get out and party – if you can find someone willing to join in.

8 MONDAY
Moon Age Day 29   Moon Sign Virgo

Your concern now turns towards orderliness in the workplace. It's clear that at the moment you want things to be just so and you won't have a great deal of patience with anyone who seems to be throwing a spanner in the works. In a social sense your tidy mind is put to good use in sorting out the mess created by a friend.

9 TUESDAY
Moon Age Day 0   Moon Sign Libra

You tend to meet obstacles of any sort with patience and a good sense of humour, which is probably more than can be said for certain other people in your vicinity. Most of the time you could feel that you have to rely on yourself and that those around you are not working efficiently or sensibly. Continue to offer support.

10 WEDNESDAY   *Moon Age Day 1   Moon Sign Libra*

Look out for the chance to make new friends, as well as ways of strengthening personal ties. Not everyone is going to be on your side in practical matters, but you have winning ways and a very persuasive nature at this time. On the rare occasion when you can't bring others round to your point of view, carry on with what you believe in anyway.

11 THURSDAY   *Moon Age Day 2   Moon Sign Scorpio*

If there are changes coming along in your working environment you should take these on board and even welcome them if you can. Virgo, like all Earth signs, tends to stick to what it knows but this can be a negative reaction sometimes. You need to be progressive and to embrace new technologies and improved techniques.

12 FRIDAY   *Moon Age Day 3   Moon Sign Scorpio*

You should have a positive and compromising attitude today, which makes others instinctively trust and like you. Popularity is not too hard for the average Virgo to find, even if you sometimes think you are not all that well loved by friends. What you always need is more self-confidence, which is present in your chart today.

13 SATURDAY   *Moon Age Day 4   Moon Sign Sagittarius*

Extended talks and general negotiations seem to be the order of the day. Some of these will prove to be very useful, while others don't offer quite the rewards you may have been expecting. Treat each situation on its own merits and don't be too alarmed if some people appear to be quite disruptive. Things can be sorted out.

14 SUNDAY   *Moon Age Day 5   Moon Sign Sagittarius*

Ideas, plans and thoughts should flow smoothly between yourself and others. This would therefore be an excellent time for working in partnerships or for getting involved in new ventures that involve colleagues. Friends also have some good ideas and you will probably want to be involved in these from the start.

15 MONDAY   *Moon Age Day 6   Moon Sign Capricorn*

At this time you are a very creative person and you can best satisfy your own personal goals by trying new things. You will want to be surrounded by order and, if possible, luxury, something that is always close to the Virgo heart. You may also be keen to make some changes at home, alongside family members.

16 TUESDAY   *Moon Age Day 7   Moon Sign Capricorn*

There could be some slight difficulties at work today. Maybe you are not communicating as well with others as would normally be the case. Have some patience in your dealings with other people, a few of whom could appear to be playing rather silly games. Socially, life should be secure enough.

17 WEDNESDAY   *Moon Age Day 8   Moon Sign Capricorn*

There is good potential for attracting new people into your life, either at work or socially. The middle of the working week is quite likely to bring you into contact with types who can be of specific use to you practically, though by the evening you will be opting to let your hair down and have some fun.

18 THURSDAY   *Moon Age Day 9   Moon Sign Aquarius*

You should have little or no trouble staying in the good books of others today. You are popular with others and it appears that you know exactly what to say in order to get the right sort of reactions. Campaigns that you have embarked upon need dealing with very carefully. Don't rush into anything.

19 FRIDAY   *Moon Age Day 10   Moon Sign Aquarius*

Socially speaking you are now likely to be drawn to the new and unusual in life. Not that there is all that much time to take notice of it today. Life is hectic, probably because of the needs that others have of you. There are moments when rules and regulations could get on your nerves if you can't find ways to ignore them.

20 SATURDAY
Moon Age Day 11   Moon Sign Pisces

This is a time during which you are challenged to overcome negative thinking and that's fine, but make sure you bear in mind that so many of your plans might not look all that workable over the next couple of days. Don't take any prohibitive action until later and, in the meantime, try to let things ride if you can.

21 SUNDAY
Moon Age Day 12   Moon Sign Pisces

It could seem that no matter how hard you try, you are getting nowhere fast. This is because you continue to knock your head against a very unnecessary wall. Stand and watch on the riverbank of life, rather than jumping into the water. The more you relax, the better you will deal with these slightly negative circumstances.

22 MONDAY
Moon Age Day 13   Moon Sign Pisces

Though group and co-operative ventures tend to go smoothly enough today, it is in the direction of personal relationships that your mind turns. Mixing freely with your friends, you could discover that one or two of them hold a key that can open some very interesting doors for you.

23 TUESDAY
Moon Age Day 14   Moon Sign Aries

There are some wonderful surprises in store for Virgo today, but you will have to keep your eye on the ball to gain from any of them. Trends indicate that not everyone is on your side in the workplace, but those who are not probably have something to gain from opposing you. Don't rise to the bait!

24 WEDNESDAY
Moon Age Day 15   Moon Sign Aries

You definitely enjoy being busy today and can make the best out of almost any sort of circumstance. Watch out for the odd minor mishap, probably brought about as a result of carelessness exhibited by someone else. Your present quick thinking makes you good to have around in any tight corner.

25 THURSDAY   *Moon Age Day 16   Moon Sign Taurus*

Now is the time to be enjoying good social trends and to be letting people know just how capable you are. It may not be particularly easy to control all aspects of your life, but you care less about certain issues at this time. Your insight into relationships should help them to work out particularly well.

26 FRIDAY   *Moon Age Day 17   Moon Sign Taurus*

Right now, making up your mind regarding even a crucial personal matter is not going to be at all easy. It might be best to defer decisions until later. By that time you will have had the chance to seek out the advice of someone you trust implicitly. Friends are easy to make at this time, and are not likely to be lost later.

27 SATURDAY   *Moon Age Day 18   Moon Sign Gemini*

Talks with others can find you making the sort of headway you hadn't been expecting. For many Virgos this is a day of rest, but this may not appeal to you on this particular Saturday. As a result, don't be surprised to find yourself out of bed early and anxious to get on with life just as quickly as you are able.

28 SUNDAY   *Moon Age Day 19   Moon Sign Gemini*

You may discover that some people are far less assertive than usual, and you can put that down to your own attitude. It is a fact that you don't brook any interference right now and that those around you get the message. The more you get done very early today, the greater is the likelihood that you can enjoy a peaceful Sunday.

29 MONDAY   *Moon Age Day 20   Moon Sign Cancer*

Emotions could be quite close to the surface now, which is a state of affairs Virgo does not like too much. Although you are generally warm, the innermost workings of your nature tend to be hidden. Feeling like a sheet of glass is not especially comfortable for anyone born under your zodiac sign.

30 TUESDAY *Moon Age Day 21   Moon Sign Cancer*

A friend or social contact is likely to be trying your patience now. It would be good to spread your influence socially and there is certainly no need to fall out with anyone. Social trends remain generally good but it's likely that you will be turning more and more to family members in order to fill your quiet hours at present.

31 WEDNESDAY *Moon Age Day 22   Moon Sign Cancer*

There are some curious situations around at the moment and since you wish to resolve them, a little detective work may be in order. Make certain that you are not wasting time on needless distractions because there is enough to do now without going down pointless roads. Scrutinise carefully any documents that need signing.

November
2018

1 THURSDAY
Moon Age Day 23   Moon Sign Leo

You could now be sensing some fairly inevitable changes in your life and it would be good if you were the one deciding what should alter. Think deeply about certain aspects and take advice from people in the know. Trends indicate that November may be a very eventful month for you.

2 FRIDAY
Moon Age Day 24   Moon Sign Leo

Your creativity may be enhanced now and whether you are working or not this Friday, you want to make things look and feel beautiful. Enlisting the support of family members, and especially your partner, should be fairly easy and together you can enjoy whatever you are doing. A trip away from your home environment seems likely.

3 SATURDAY
Moon Age Day 25   Moon Sign Virgo

Look around carefully because a word in the right ear can work virtual miracles at present. Give yourself fully to all that the day has to offer, particularly if you awaken with a feeling of concern that things may not be going your way. Making progress in matters of the heart and really enjoying yourself are what today is about.

4 SUNDAY
Moon Age Day 26   Moon Sign Virgo

You will be able to take full advantage of almost any situation now. With friends willing to do what they can to assist, you embark on a distinctly social day, with plenty of enjoyment possible and some financial gains also in evidence. Don't be tardy when it comes to expressing an opinion.

5 MONDAY
Moon Age Day 27   Moon Sign Libra

The accent today is more or less totally on fun and pleasure, even if you have to go to work. You can make any situation enjoyable and will want to involve others in many of your zany schemes. Virgo is light-hearted and fun-loving in almost everything now and it will be quite difficult for you to take any aspect of life completely seriously.

6 TUESDAY
Moon Age Day 28   Moon Sign Libra

Your main focus now remains on doing what you can to help others, though your attitude isn't entirely charitable because you are doing yourself some good on the way. Have some fun during today and get together with like-minded people whenever you can. You should also find time to show how romantic you are.

7 WEDNESDAY
Moon Age Day 0   Moon Sign Scorpio

Your generally contented outlook on life makes you popular with just about everyone today and allows you to push the bounds of the possible when it comes to getting those around you to do what you want. A little cheek can go a long way and you could end up very surprised at just how much you can influence people.

8 THURSDAY
Moon Age Day 1   Moon Sign Scorpio

You are a natural detective as you seek to ferret out the truth. Today can be interesting and useful when it comes to discovering what is really going on around you and there could be some surprises regarding the behaviour of a family member or a friend. In the main you should be fairly happy and contented with your own lot.

9 FRIDAY
Moon Age Day 2   Moon Sign Sagittarius

Virgo is on form and it is now easy for you to shine in personal matters, during a period that is excellent regarding your closest attachments. Where there has been a little discord, now you find reconciliation and warmth. It may not be your own attitude that has changed at all but rather the ideas and opinions of others.

10 SATURDAY   *Moon Age Day 3   Moon Sign Sagittarius*

Things just seem to get better. Friendship and group encounters generally appear to have a great deal going for them right now. What they provide is a platform for your ego, perhaps at a time when you are not quite as confident in yourself as has been the case of late. Make time to socialise, particularly by the evening.

11 SUNDAY   *Moon Age Day 4   Moon Sign Sagittarius*

It looks as though consolidation is the key to getting on well right now. Instead of firing off with new ideas, look carefully at the ones you have been addressing recently. It might take only a very small amount of effort to put the seal on weeks or months of work. On the way through life today new friends are a possibility.

12 MONDAY   *Moon Age Day 5   Moon Sign Capricorn*

Everyday issues should keep you happily on the go today and although this time may not be exactly startling as far as you are concerned, it should be reasonably enjoyable. Try not to allow yourself to be bogged down by details that don't matter and avoid worrying about people who are doing fine. Keep up new efforts

13 TUESDAY   *Moon Age Day 6   Moon Sign Capricorn*

You can be a definite agent for change today if you apply yourself properly. You are a natural reformer and can do things now that will improve the lot of others, as well as having a significant bearing on your own life. Where money is concerned you could have been fairly conservative recently, but should be more of a gambler now.

14 WEDNESDAY   *Moon Age Day 7   Moon Sign Aquarius*

This would be a very fortunate time for business discussions and for making alterations to the way you do things in a practical sense. It could be that you now recognise you have been chasing some sort of rainbow recently. This leads to more concerted action and a definite change of emphasis now and for the days to come.

15 THURSDAY *Moon Age Day 8 Moon Sign Aquarius*

Now you are constantly looking for new opportunities and showing the world at large just how savvy you have. It should still be easy to get others to back you in your schemes and you have a great deal of resolve when dealing with those in authority. The occasional shyness of Virgo is definitely not on display right now.

16 FRIDAY *Moon Age Day 9 Moon Sign Aquarius*

Your social life might be something of a letdown at the moment. If so, you probably are not dealing with certain people in the right way. Certainly you should not allow yourself to be held back by negative attitudes. Leave alone those individuals who insist on taking a pessimistic approach to life.

17 SATURDAY ☿ *Moon Age Day 10 Moon Sign Pisces*

It would not be in the least surprising to find that you lack energy today or that you cannot get yourself motivated in the way you wish. Let others do some of the hard work, while you sit back and supervise. You are still making your own choices and as far as your determination is concerned very little seems to have changed.

18 SUNDAY ☿ *Moon Age Day 11 Moon Sign Pisces*

It is likely that you will feel pulled in different directions today. Your loyalty lies in more than one place and so deciding who you should please may not be easy. While the Moon is in Pisces it is probably best not to try. You are not quite as ingenious right now as you have been, or as you will be in the days ahead.

19 MONDAY ☿ *Moon Age Day 12 Moon Sign Aries*

Along comes a day for positive social relations and one that finds you distinctly more up front than appears to have been the case yesterday. Sort out any routines early in the day and don't be afraid to have some fun. Others may notice how much you tease at present, but this is hardly likely to be a stumbling block.

20 TUESDAY ☿ Moon Age Day 13 Moon Sign Aries

When things get quiet, Virgos might spend time pampering themselves. Why not? You have put in a great deal of effort in the recent past and you deserve to have a decent rest. If, on the other hand, you have to work today, do as little as you can and allow others to fill in where possible. This could be a fairly uneventful day.

21 WEDNESDAY ☿ Moon Age Day 14 Moon Sign Taurus

You will most likely actively choose to be on the move during the course of your daily affairs for the moment. Staying in one place and doing exactly what is expected of you is hardly likely to be much fun and there is so much scope for having a good time it seems rather pointless to restrict yourself unduly.

22 THURSDAY ☿ Moon Age Day 15 Moon Sign Taurus

Career matters that lack direction should be dealt with firmly and immediately right now. Don't let things stew in your life generally and be willing to take the sort of decisions that you know to be sensible. Your attitude towards loved ones varies, especially if some of them are being deliberately awkward.

23 FRIDAY ☿ Moon Age Day 16 Moon Sign Taurus

Your social life could prove to be rather testy and this means that you have to question certain relationships and what they are presently offering you. Try to examine the overall effect you are having on others, but don't judge yourself too harshly. In all situations those around you can be wrong, too.

24 SATURDAY ☿ Moon Age Day 17 Moon Sign Gemini

Your persuasive powers over others are pretty strong today, so if there is anything you really want, now is the time to go out and ask for it. It won't be as simple as that of course, though nobody you care for will refuse reasonable requests. Socially speaking you seem to be reaching a high and may be planning ahead well.

25 SUNDAY ☿ *Moon Age Day 18   Moon Sign Gemini*

The pursuit of wealth might now be on your list of priorities. Virgo may not be the most acquisitive of the zodiac signs, but it isn't too far behind. It's all down to a sense of security, which Virgo desires. Casting your mind forward in time, you can now do some deals that will suit your needs in years to come.

26 MONDAY ☿ *Moon Age Day 19   Moon Sign Cancer*

Stay clear of disagreements today if you can possibly manage to do so. It would be better not to interact too much with people at all, rather than to find yourself involved in pointless rows. Such a state of affairs is far less likely in terms of deep attachments. Virgos who are looking for love should have some success now.

27 TUESDAY ☿ *Moon Age Day 20   Moon Sign Cancer*

Compromise is your middle name today, or at least it if isn't, then it should be. You can get more today by being willing to give a little than at just about any other time this month. Some nostalgia creeps in, but that is part of the way present trends make themselves felt in your life. Soon you will be flying high again.

28 WEDNESDAY ☿ *Moon Age Day 21   Moon Sign Leo*

On a practical level, you are quite pressured, but this fact will not prevent you from getting on well all the same. Out here in the middle of the week, and in the midst of some demanding situations, there are people who buckle under the pressure. You, fortunately, are not one of them. Give what support you can.

29 THURSDAY ☿ *Moon Age Day 22   Moon Sign Leo*

Social encounters look good and are inclined to inspire you to try new possibilities. There are opportunities to meet people who may be in a good position to offer you advice and the association you have with others at this time could start your mind thinking along lines that haven't been available in the past.

30 FRIDAY ☿ *Moon Age Day 23   Moon Sign Virgo*

Changing solar influences come along now that stimulate your natural curiosity regarding the world and the way it runs. It would be sensible to allow professionals, or people you feel to be superior, to know of your own thoughts today. Even the most casual remarks you make are likely to be taken on board.

December
2018

1 SATURDAY   ☿   *Moon Age Day 24   Moon Sign Virgo*

This Saturday puts a spring in your step and a smile firmly on your face. The fact is that with the lunar high about you are the life and soul of any party. Friends and relatives alike seem to be doing all they can to make you happy now, though most of the effort is clearly coming from your direction.

2 SUNDAY   ☿   *Moon Age Day 25   Moon Sign Libra*

You may now be in discussion regarding an emotional matter and it's a fact that much of what is happening today will be associated with your home. Things can be solved quite easily just as long as you are willing to talk and with Mercury in its present position that should hardly be a problem.

3 MONDAY   ☿   *Moon Age Day 26   Moon Sign Libra*

Someone might be trying to put you down in the minds of others, or at least that's how it will appear to you right now. It is likely that you are not looking at things quite as logically as would normally be the case and emotions can get in the way. Most importantly, keep a smile on your face, even when you feel jumpy.

4 TUESDAY   ☿   *Moon Age Day 27   Moon Sign Scorpio*

It seems as though you will be looking for a more advantageous social position as you entertain others and keep people smiling throughout most of today. You generally have an interesting story to tell and it won't be hard for you to maintain your standing as the centre of attention. Your personal life should take a turn for the better now.

5 WEDNESDAY ☿ *Moon Age Day 28 Moon Sign Scorpio*

Self-determination on your part paves the way towards achieving personal goals around this time. Put your best foot forward in all practical matters especially and show the world just how capable you can be. Later in the day you should find that the romantic responses coming your way are not quite what you expected.

6 THURSDAY ☿ *Moon Age Day 29 Moon Sign Scorpio*

Today's personal news may put you nicely in touch with the wider world and this in turn reminds you of concerns that exist a long way from your own front door. You become a more charitable animal at this time of year and will want to do what you can to help those who are less well off than you are. Virgo is definitely a caring sign at present.

7 FRIDAY *Moon Age Day 0 Moon Sign Sagittarius*

Today could be a good time to focus on the very practical aspects of life. Roll up your sleeves and get cracking this Friday, sorting out all those issues that have been left on the shelf for a while. It's part of clearing the decks ahead of the holidays and it is something that Virgo is inclined to do regularly at this time of year.

8 SATURDAY *Moon Age Day 1 Moon Sign Sagittarius*

You tend to be quite outspoken now, so if you are involved in discussions it is possible that you will have to guard your tongue. Speaking out of turn now could bring problems further down the road. The right sort of circumstances to allow material progress may not be present at first, but they may develop later.

9 SUNDAY *Moon Age Day 2 Moon Sign Capricorn*

It looks as though challenges will come along at this time, though most of them are welcome since they offer you the chance to show exactly what you are made of. The objections that others might make about your life may only serve to show where their own faults lie. For this reason alone it isn't worth rising to the bait.

10 MONDAY
Moon Age Day 3   Moon Sign Capricorn

Since you need to express yourself fully now there's a chance you will be so busy talking that you will overlook a few fairly important details. This isn't like you as a rule, but then nobody is perfect! What might really get your goat at the moment are rules and regulations for which you can see no real justification.

11 TUESDAY
Moon Age Day 4   Moon Sign Aquarius

Matters of the heart should be a genuine source of support and happiness today. Although this means that you may not be keeping your eye on the ball as much as usual in a practical sense, all should be well in your world as a whole. Some forward planning regarding the holiday season can now be addressed.

12 WEDNESDAY
Moon Age Day 5   Moon Sign Aquarius

Socially speaking you could now find yourself entering a short lull. Others are grumpy or difficult to deal with and a great deal of patience is necessary. On the other hand you could choose instead to spend a few hours on your own. Those born under the sign of Virgo are quite happy to go it alone now and then.

13 THURSDAY
Moon Age Day 6   Moon Sign Aquarius

Things change and socially speaking you ought to be fairly impressive now. There are plenty of people around on whom you can try out your present skills and since most of them appear to care for you the job should be easy. However, you might find that it is more of a problem to deal with arising difficulties at work.

14 FRIDAY
Moon Age Day 7   Moon Sign Pisces

If there are challenges in emotional relationships just now you can thank the lunar low for them. Nothing that happens at present is likely to shake your equilibrium too much and your forgiving nature is still very much present. It might be best not to push yourself too hard and to be willing to take a little rest right now.

15 SATURDAY
Moon Age Day 8   Moon Sign Pisces

It could feel as if you are not totally in charge of your own destiny at this stage of the week and that can make you rather uncertain and somewhat hesitant. Don't worry because these trends are very temporary. By tomorrow you should be right back on form, but for the moment you may have to rely more heavily on other people.

16 SUNDAY
Moon Age Day 9   Moon Sign Pisces

Today you tend to feel very sociable and easy-going as the worst excesses of the lunar low disappear completely. With Christmas firmly in your sights you will be socialising a lot more than might have been the case earlier in the month and it also looks as though you will be quite busy in every practical sense at the moment.

17 MONDAY
Moon Age Day 10   Moon Sign Aries

What an ideal time this is to be out there in the social mainstream of life. Parties and gatherings of any sort appeal to you because you are presently the life and soul of any function. However, be careful how much you eat and drink because otherwise you may end up regretting your tendency towards excess.

18 TUESDAY
Moon Age Day 11   Moon Sign Aries

Along comes a time for capitalising on all recent advances at work. It really is time to strike while the iron is hot and to do things before Christmas actually arrives. In a family sense not everyone is likely to be equally helpful and many of the everyday responsibilities appear to be falling on you.

19 WEDNESDAY
Moon Age Day 12   Moon Sign Taurus

Your approach to certain emotional matters might not be as positive as you had first intended. If this turns out to be the case you will simply have to try again. Realising that you are capable of getting it wrong is the first step on an important inward journey. Social trends still look good and enjoyment is on the cards.

20 THURSDAY *Moon Age Day 13   Moon Sign Taurus*

Any number of speculative matters could turn your way right now and you can afford to take the odd little chance in life. As the day wears on, it is likely that you will be running out of steam physically, though it's clear that your mind is working well and that you are in a position to offer some sound advice.

21 FRIDAY *Moon Age Day 14   Moon Sign Gemini*

Compromises in relationships are a natural part of what you will encounter at the present time. If you refuse to make them, problems could come along later. Stay away from rows in your family, or indeed amongst friends. The problem is not one of failing to hold your own, but rather being too aggressive.

22 SATURDAY *Moon Age Day 15   Moon Sign Gemini*

Get ready to make tracks and get ahead professionally. With one eye on Christmas and the other on what you want to achieve materially, there isn't a great deal of time to spare right now. Don't overbook yourself for the forthcoming days. There may be shopping to do today that you had forgotten.

23 SUNDAY *Moon Age Day 16   Moon Sign Cancer*

Getting along with others isn't too difficult this Sunday, just as long as they are willing to do more or less exactly what you ask. The fact is that you are being rather more selfish than would normally be the case. Get out and about if you can, though it is likely that your main destination will still be the local shopping centre.

24 MONDAY *Moon Age Day 17   Moon Sign Cancer*

The emotional rewards from intimate relationships are showing much more clearly now. Your confidence rises as you realise that people are really listening to what you have to say. Go for what you want and be willing to grab the odd chance that under normal circumstances you may shy away from.

25 TUESDAY

Moon Age Day 18   Moon Sign Leo

You should definitely be feeling at your best today. The people who matter the most are around you and Christmas Day has much to offer in terms of genuine warmth and affection. Don't forget obligations to those who can't be with you at this time and remain at your charitable best generally.

26 WEDNESDAY

Moon Age Day 19   Moon Sign Leo

Social developments are now positively highlighted, allowing you to make the most of the time between now and the New Year. Virgo becomes quite the party animal and you know how to help others to have a good time too. The everyday responsibilities of life are now shelved.

27 THURSDAY

Moon Age Day 20   Moon Sign Virgo

It cannot get much better than having the lunar high present during the Christmas holidays. You should be filled with beans and anxious to get as much out of life as you possibly can. People will warm to your infectious humour and to the fact that you put yourself out so much on their behalf. This should be a really good day.

28 FRIDAY

Moon Age Day 21   Moon Sign Virgo

This is the best part of the month for fresh starts and for getting ahead with unfinished work. Everything goes with a swing now and you can impress people as easily as falling off a log. Your popularity ought to be high and because you are not in the mood for work you will certainly show others that you know how to have a good time.

29 SATURDAY

Moon Age Day 22   Moon Sign Libra

Stick to the simple things of life and spend some time spoiling yourself. There is an active and very demanding period ahead, so it won't do you any harm to charge up those batteries. Your confidence should not be dented unless you come face to face with people who seem determined to put you down.

30 SUNDAY
Moon Age Day 23   Moon Sign Libra

Things remain generally positive. You score many points in social situations, especially so if you are away from home and enjoying the hospitality of others. Try not to be critical about the way those around you arrange their functions and simply pitch in. Too much fussing won't get you anywhere today so try to stay very relaxed.

31 MONDAY
Moon Age Day 24   Moon Sign Libra

New Year's Eve brings you to thinking quite deeply about what you have achieved and you will also be carefully planning what comes next. That's fine during the day but by the time the evening arrives you will have other things to do. Enjoy whatever party you go to and stay in the company of people who you care for deeply.

VIRGO:
2019 DIARY PAGES

VIRGO:
YOUR YEAR IN BRIEF

The year should get off to a fairly good start, even if you can't get everything you really want from life. January has its drawbacks, though these could have as much to do with the time of year as with any adverse astrological trend. Finances should be reasonably strong and tend to remain so throughout much of February. You are planning carefully and all you really lack at this time is the sort of excitement that might pep up your life no end.

March and April continue the generally favourable trends and bring you slightly closer to some of your heart's desires. This may not be the best time of the year as far as the weather is concerned, but you can build your own warmth in the way you treat others and feel it in the love that comes back to you in response. Don't get bogged down with irrelevant details at this time.

As summer blooms, May and June get you thinking about all those plans you had at the beginning of the year – a few of which are now likely to be put into action. Everything comes to those who wait and Virgo is certainly no exception. Now you begin to benefit from the patience and effort you put in earlier. Look out for new chances at work and fresh starts at home.

Now comes the time when you really start to motor. The high summer is a period when you will sparkle. July and August should find you willing to take more chances and in a good position to benefit from the support of others. All should be well in your relationships and love is in the air for many Virgos at this time. Keep a sense of proportion socially speaking but grasp at any chance for travel that comes your way.

You continue to be active during the autumn period. September and October will see you doing everything you can to make life go with a swing and there are plenty of people around who would be willing to join in with any of your plans. This would also be a good time for travel and for convincing family members that change is not necessarily a bad thing. That's rich coming from Virgo, though for some reason you are freewheeling now.

November and December should be both useful and heart-warming in a number of different ways. New friendships are possible and you are committed to changes in and out of your home. You won't make much allowance for the winter weather and could be travelling more than usual. Christmas is likely to be happy and active and the New Year promises more of the same in terms of general forward progress.

January

2019

1 TUESDAY
Moon Age Day 25   Moon Sign Scorpio

However long a particular task takes is the time you have to spend on it. That is self-evident to you, but may not be to other people. There is a deep and profound spirituality about your thinking on this New Year's Day, which is probably why others may be seeking you out for help and advice.

2 WEDNESDAY
Moon Age Day 26   Moon Sign Scorpio

A professional matter now proves to be very uplifting as you discover the right way to go about a particular task that might have been something of a mystery to you before. Concentration becomes easier as you settle down to accepting that this is a now a new year and that, consequently, this could be the time to make a change.

3 THURSDAY
Moon Age Day 27   Moon Sign Sagittarius

It may appear that this is a good time to sit and think about the good old days. Nostalgia is fine and has its place in our emotional suitcase, but it probably doesn't help you too much as a rule and it is certainly not likely to now. Try some forward thinking and enjoy the positive prospects you find around you at this time.

4 FRIDAY
Moon Age Day 28   Moon Sign Sagittarius

It may now be difficult to bend career situations the way you would wish and so it might be best not to try, at least for the moment. Concentrating on the matter at hand won't be too easy either, so be aware of the broader view in any situation. Something or someone unusual may come into your world soon.

5 SATURDAY   *Moon Age Day 0   Moon Sign Capricorn*

You need to be aware of the possibility of being driven by emotionally based habits now, something that can happen to Virgo from time to time. Look for new possibilities in your life and be willing to go with the flow, even if that sometimes appears to be the wrong direction. A good time for change.

6 SUNDAY   *Moon Age Day 1   Moon Sign Capricorn*

The simpler side of life appeals to you most on this Sunday. Although the weather probably isn't too good and the days are short, you might benefit from some time spent in the fresh air. A healthier sort of Virgo now begins to emerge and more of the outdoors could form part of your strategy.

7 MONDAY   *Moon Age Day 2   Moon Sign Capricorn*

It could be said that getting what you want from life today is more important than almost anything else. Unfortunately, this makes you sound a little selfish, which isn't the case at all. On the contrary, most of what you want involves a better life for others, even if you do help yourself on the way.

8 TUESDAY   *Moon Age Day 3   Moon Sign Aquarius*

The more the merrier is the adage today, both in terms of the jobs you are taking on and with regard to the number of people you are entertaining in your life, whether you know them or not. Your communication skills are good and you should be able to come to terms with a few past errors.

9 WEDNESDAY   *Moon Age Day 4   Moon Sign Aquarius*

Get out and about as much as you can today. It does you good to mix and mingle with others, despite the winter weather. In any case a change is as good as a rest, particularly if that means you are coming together with the sort of people who find you very attractive. Concentrate on money matters later in the day.

10 THURSDAY
Moon Age Day 5   Moon Sign Pisces

It seems to be time to slow down and to take a break. You might be feeling somewhat lacking in lustre and if this is the case you can blame the position of the Moon. Lunar lows are not usually too much of a problem to Virgo, however, which as a sign is inclined to retreat into itself on occasion in any case.

11 FRIDAY
Moon Age Day 6   Moon Sign Pisces

Issues in the practical world ought to be going your way now, though you may need to pay attention to little details and the sort of very careful view of which Virgo is definitely more than capable. You may get a great deal more done than you actually expect, particularly with some proffered help.

12 SATURDAY
Moon Age Day 7   Moon Sign Pisces

This is a forward-looking period and one that finds you much more in the mainstream of life. Rushing on towards specific objectives, it is clear that you know what you want from life and how to go about getting it. Try to make your home comfortable and listen to family members who have an important tale to tell.

13 SUNDAY
Moon Age Day 8   Moon Sign Aries

Others might see this as a fairly self-indulgent time for Virgo. This is a part of your personality that crops up time and again, and is partly the reason why Virgoans often have to watch what they eat. You have no real tendency towards selfishness, but you can sometimes be short of confidence. Don't turn to short-term solutions.

14 MONDAY
Moon Age Day 9   Moon Sign Aries

A personal matter needs extra patience and the sort of overview that you are able to offer. Much of your thinking is now geared towards house and home, with the result that the more practical aspects could be taking a back seat. You may decide that the time is right to brush up your life, perhaps in terms of personal fitness.

15 TUESDAY   *Moon Age Day 10   Moon Sign Taurus*

Large gatherings appeal to you at the moment. Socially or professionally, it seems that you are in full flow and your powers of communication are emphasised as a result. This isn't the time you would choose to take a day away from work, though you might tend to burn the candle at both ends more than is good for you.

16 WEDNESDAY   *Moon Age Day 11   Moon Sign Taurus*

Work and practical matters are on a much firmer footing now than might have seemed to be the case earlier. Friends should be supportive and kind and you could discover that you have a few pals you didn't know about. Confirm your suspicions regarding a certain person by asking a few leading and important questions.

17 THURSDAY   *Moon Age Day 12   Moon Sign Taurus*

You should get the emotional support you need today even if you have to look for it and ask someone outright. In your current charming mood, people can refuse you nothing. Travel, even just short distances, really appeals to you and helps you to display your very best Virgoan qualities.

18 FRIDAY   *Moon Age Day 13   Moon Sign Gemini*

When it comes to expanding your interests today, you can be sure that communication with others is going to be very important. In any situation it is essential to argue for your strengths and not your limitations. Have confidence in the advice you get from family members because what you hear is sound.

19 SATURDAY   *Moon Age Day 14   Moon Sign Gemini*

Social contacts are very important today and you are amassing a good deal of useful information that is going to serve you well in practical as well as social ways. As creative as ever, you want to make your home look good and will likely be laying down plans for your activities in the weeks ahead.

20 SUNDAY
Moon Age Day 15   Moon Sign Cancer

Emotional matters can be quite up and down at this time, which is why you are more likely to concentrate on simple friendships. This Sunday could be a mixture of practical matters, such as beautifying your home, and social interludes that bring an important element of joy into the next two days.

21 MONDAY
Moon Age Day 16   Moon Sign Cancer

You will not be happy to be steeped in mundane responsibilities today and will take greater delight in being able to choose what you do for yourself. The attitude of friends can be somewhat difficult to understand and you might have to go to great lengths to find out what is troubling them. Your natural Virgoan patience will be a boon.

22 TUESDAY
Moon Age Day 17   Moon Sign Leo

It is likely to be the professional area of your life that is best supported by present astrological trends, though you need to balance this with the fact the personal attachments are proving to be a little complicated. Socially speaking, you would be better mixing with friends and colleagues today rather than family members.

23 WEDNESDAY
Moon Age Day 18   Moon Sign Leo

Success levels in professional matters improve noticeably in the middle of this working week. Conforming to expectations in more personal matters isn't as easy and takes some thinking about. Family members should prove to be very supportive and can offer sound advice when it matters the most.

24 THURSDAY
Moon Age Day 19   Moon Sign Virgo

The Moon is in your zodiac sign. That means a get-up-and-go sort of period and one that is typified by high levels of energy and an irrepressible desire to be out there in the mainstream of life. In terms of experiences, quality is as important as quantity, though you should manage to get a little of both today.

25 FRIDAY
Moon Age Day 20   Moon Sign Virgo

Future plans can give you a shot in the arm with the weekend just around the corner. In fact, most of you will be finishing the working week with a flourish and though not all news appears to be good, you can get the best from all of it. Rummage around to find clothes that you can put back into service because you are ingenious now.

26 SATURDAY
Moon Age Day 21   Moon Sign Libra

Maybe you are less sensitive to the remarks of others than has been the case of late and you certainly appear to be treating many matters as a joke, which has to be good. Friends will find you supportive and fun to have around. Some tasks will have to be dealt with a little at a time and using a degree of ingenuity.

27 SUNDAY
Moon Age Day 22   Moon Sign Libra

You will be taking as many chances as you can to expand your horizons today and won't easily be put off by negative types, a few of whom could emerge at the moment. Because you are so naturally cheerful, your state of mind rubs off on others, who will show themselves anxious to join in the fun.

28 MONDAY
Moon Age Day 23   Moon Sign Scorpio

The more ambitious you show yourself to be today, the greater is the support you will get from others. Arguments should be strenuously avoided, particularly at home and it seems clear that you are out to enjoy yourself as much as possible. An over-serious attitude is something you will not look for.

29 TUESDAY
Moon Age Day 24   Moon Sign Scorpio

Practical matters will probably get off to a slow start today, which is why it could seem as though you are chasing your tail for the majority of the working day. When professional and practical concerns are out of the way, there should be an opportunity to enjoy yourself, which you will grasp with both hands.

30 WEDNESDAY *Moon Age Day 25*   *Moon Sign Sagittarius*

You may feel a real wanderlust right now and really would not be happy sticking around home all the time. It is a fact that your happiness at present exists in direct proportion to the amount of change and diversity that is coming into your life. Much of this has to be found by you, though you will want to share your excitement with others.

31 THURSDAY   *Moon Age Day 26*   *Moon Sign Sagittarius*

You can't please all of the people all of the time at present and there really isn't very much mileage in trying to do so. Life can be quite interesting in some ways but distinctly tedious in others. It's up to you to sort the wheat from the chaff and to give yourself room to change your mind.

February 2019

1 FRIDAY
Moon Age Day 27   Moon Sign Sagittarius

It's true that you have to work quite hard now to get the good things of life, but being a Virgoan that doesn't worry you too much. Look out for the help and support of friends, some of whom have a good idea or two that in the fullness of time could make you significantly better off than you are now.

2 SATURDAY
Moon Age Day 28   Moon Sign Capricorn

Though you are more than ready to form new contacts of one sort or another today, you should avoid coming on too strong in certain situations. Confidence is important, but you must avoid giving people the wrong impression. A healthy dose of your natural humility does more for you now than a brash approach.

3 SUNDAY
Moon Age Day 29   Moon Sign Capricorn

In a career sense, situations are beginning to improve, though it could be difficult to monitor the situation if you don't work on a Sunday. This would be a good day for shopping or for spending some time in the company of lively and articulate friends. What you don't need at the moment are grumpy types.

4 MONDAY
Moon Age Day 0   Moon Sign Aquarius

Getting ahead today depends on a degree of specialised knowledge, which in one form or another we all have. Ask yourself what you know about that others do not and concentrate on those matters. Somewhere within them lies an ability to get on better and to make more money. Be supportive of friends who are in trouble.

5 TUESDAY
Moon Age Day 1   Moon Sign Aquarius

You might register the fact that things are not working out entirely as you would wish. An extra dose of self-created enthusiasm gets you through any minor difficulties now and there are new incentives coming your way before the day is out. The most promising aspects of your life are social in nature.

6 WEDNESDAY
Moon Age Day 2   Moon Sign Aquarius

Although many of the opportunities that come your way today prove to be small in scope, the end result of them is likely to prove very positive. It is all a matter of looking carefully and then concentrating on one task a time. No matter how unlikely it looks, you can exert a greater influence over your own life now.

7 THURSDAY
Moon Age Day 3   Moon Sign Pisces

Try to shelve any big plans if possible today. The Moon is in your opposite zodiac sign which means that you should not be taking on matters that are going to tax you too much. Your confidence is a little dented, but you can get enjoyment from simple things and from the company of those you love.

8 FRIDAY
Moon Age Day 4   Moon Sign Pisces

You cannot get away entirely from the presence of the lunar low today. For a sign such as yours, the position of the Moon in your opposite zodiac sign is not always particularly noticeable. However, you may feel that life is not proceeding quite as smoothly as has recently been the case and extra effort is required.

9 SATURDAY
Moon Age Day 5   Moon Sign Aries

Trends move on and this is now a time of high spirits. Things that are going on in the outside world should lift your spirits nicely. Freedom is the key to happiness and you will find yourself able to get through or over obstacles that have blocked your path for quite some time. What helps is that you are now being so realistic.

10 SUNDAY
Moon Age Day 6   Moon Sign Aries

Social matters ought to prove highly stimulating and you can enjoy the company of a number of different sorts of people. You need to balance outside activities with pressing work obligations, in which you might be slipping behind a little. There should be plenty of time for enjoyment in the evening.

11 MONDAY
Moon Age Day 7   Moon Sign Aries

This is a very fruitful period for friendships and for finding people with whom you instinctively feel you have much in common. Some patience will be necessary regarding a specific enterprise but people probably won't keep you waiting that long. A degree of ingenuity is what's called for at this time.

12 TUESDAY
Moon Age Day 8   Moon Sign Taurus

Inside, you might be quaking at the thought of some contact or approach you now have to make, though this is absolutely necessary if you want to make more of yourself in the days and weeks ahead. Summon up all your courage and move forward. The people you might fear are by no means ogres.

13 WEDNESDAY
Moon Age Day 9   Moon Sign Taurus

If there is one area of life that doesn't look quite as happy and solid as others, it could be related to your love life. You need to have a heart to heart with your partner, or someone else who has a bearing on your emotions. You will be surprised at just how much better you feel once you have spoken your mind.

14 THURSDAY
Moon Age Day 10   Moon Sign Gemini

In the area of personal relationships, you will have to show extra special patience and tolerance. Loved ones could be behaving in a strange and unpredictable manner, often leaving you guessing. For some relief you might turn in the direction of good friends, most of whom prove to be far less complicated at present. Perhaps mark Valentine's Day at the weekend, instead?

15 FRIDAY
Moon Age Day 11   Moon Sign Gemini

Career developments are likely to continue on an upward spiral. People are listening to what you have to say and responding in a very positive manner. Contributing to your own success in a whole host of ways isn't particularly difficult and you have it within yourself to impress almost anyone you meet.

16 SATURDAY
Moon Age Day 12   Moon Sign Cancer

Most people seem to be filled with goodwill towards you today, a fact that you need to take on board if you really want to get on well. If those around you are willing to put themselves out on your behalf, it would be somewhat strange of you to snub them. Don't assume they are trying to steal your thunder in some way.

17 SUNDAY
Moon Age Day 13   Moon Sign Cancer

This may be one of your best days for bringing a particular problem to a satisfactory conclusion. Avoid family arguments, particularly ones you had no hand in starting. Slow and steady wins the race in most areas of your life, but you might be racing ahead towards the conclusion of a financial chapter.

18 MONDAY
Moon Age Day 14   Moon Sign Leo

The desires of other people can clash somewhat with the future you see for yourself. Reconciling two opposing points of view isn't going to be at all easy, though with understanding and a degree of patience, you should be able to win through. Compromise isn't the same as backing down.

19 TUESDAY
Moon Age Day 15   Moon Sign Leo

This is an excellent day on which to take advantage of situations of any sort, but particularly at work. Your powers of communication are extremely good and your intuition is honed to perfection. Spend the day working hard and then relax as fully as you can in the evening.

20 WEDNESDAY
Moon Age Day 16   Moon Sign Virgo

This can be a very good day for making progress. Special projects that are very close to your heart may receive important developments and something you have been thinking about for a while could now become a reality with financial implications. You don't really look for security today but will be in the market for excitement.

21 THURSDAY
Moon Age Day 17   Moon Sign Virgo

Although you are probably being very successful at present, there is no time for complacency. It is true that you have a superior sort of judgement but you need to use it wisely. The outcome of recent efforts allows you to make more of yourself and to show an extremely positive face to the world.

22 FRIDAY
Moon Age Day 18   Moon Sign Libra

Get out as much as possible this Friday, even if that effectively means starting the weekend a day early. A shopping expedition would definitely suit your present mood and you are willing to go that extra mile to please both family members and friends. Deal with necessary tasks in manageable chunks.

23 SATURDAY
Moon Age Day 19   Moon Sign Libra

You are turning your attention towards an important plan of action at this time, and it has got you really fired up and anxious to make the very best impression you possibly can. Don't be quick to take offence at someone who is really only speaking their mind in a way that seems right to them.

24 SUNDAY
Moon Age Day 20   Moon Sign Scorpio

Your quick thinking can prove decisive at some stage during this Sunday and it is very important to speak out at any time if you know you have a valid point of view. If you get the feeling that someone is trying to gag you, it could be that what you are saying somehow upsets their sensibilities. Try to resolve a family issue.

25 MONDAY
Moon Age Day 21   Moon Sign Scorpio

There are downsides to discussions, a fact that means you are not quite so likely to be getting on with others as you have of late. Avoid arguing, since it isn't really going to get you anywhere. It would be better to spend time on your own than to get on the wrong side of someone you know to be important.

26 TUESDAY
Moon Age Day 22   Moon Sign Sagittarius

Now would be as good a time as any to bring certain personal matters to a head. You are romantically inclined and so very unlikely to fall out with people who are close to you in a personal sense. You won't take kindly to being put into an embarrassing position and should shy away from controversy.

27 WEDNESDAY
Moon Age Day 23   Moon Sign Sagittarius

Things change and in terms of friendship you should be on a real winner today, so it is worth going those extra few steps in order to ensure that you are around the right people. Casual conversations can have far-reaching implications and no information you receive at present should be ignored.

28 THURSDAY
Moon Age Day 24   Moon Sign Sagittarius

Social invitations are likely to be coming in thick and fast at present, a sure sign that your mood is on the up. Most of these you will be happy to accept, though do remember that you can't split yourself in two and if you know you have family commitments at the moment, this could add to the pressure.

March

2019

1 FRIDAY
Moon Age Day 25   Moon Sign Capricorn

This is a beneficial phase that should bring your communication skills to the fore. With plenty going your way and life looking pretty good, you will be feeling fine and able to deal with just about any challenge that comes your way. Keep a sense of proportion over small financial losses.

2 SATURDAY
Moon Age Day 26   Moon Sign Capricorn

The accent is now on the domestic scene and you turn your attention towards matters associated with house and home. There is a long month ahead of you and for much of the time you will be very busy. As a result, you may choose to spend more time with family members, since you won't have much opportunity later.

3 SUNDAY
Moon Age Day 27   Moon Sign Aquarius

Prepare to make a rather positive impact on people who can be of great use to you later. Stay away from jobs that bore you and try to do those things that can be exciting and different. A complete change of scene would suit you down the ground, and some attractive and interesting people could notice you.

4 MONDAY
Moon Age Day 28   Moon Sign Aquarius

Some setbacks at work can be expected, but you do have the ability to turn them around. Now and again today you will find yourself up against people who seem determined to be awkward. The best way to deal with them is to show them your present charming character, which can be totally disarming.

5 TUESDAY   *Moon Age Day 29   Moon Sign Aquarius*

You are in a very positive frame of mind today and stand a chance of making a good deal of progress as a result. What might be even more important is your ability to turn heads and to make other people notice the fact that you are around. This can help you at work, but also personally, too.

6 WEDNESDAY ☿   *Moon Age Day 0   Moon Sign Pisces*

Don't expect to get all that much done today. The lunar low is inclined to get in the way and prevents you from moving forward in quite the way you might wish. If you get nervy about something you know you are going to have to say, have a little rehearsal. Even in situations where you are shaking, you can still come through.

7 THURSDAY ☿   *Moon Age Day 1   Moon Sign Pisces*

Make as much time as possible for relaxation and don't push yourself so hard you find it difficult to slow your mind down later. There is time to do almost anything you want but half a dozen jobs at the same time won't help. A good day for romance – that is if you have the time to notice and you are being observed.

8 FRIDAY ☿   *Moon Age Day 2   Moon Sign Aries*

This is one of the most pleasurable days of the month as far as social matters are concerned. If you have to work it's a pity because now you really do want to have fun. Even if you are tied down by responsibility through the day, you will be redressing the balance before very long.

9 SATURDAY ☿   *Moon Age Day 3   Moon Sign Aries*

Make sure others don't misconstrue what you are saying. Even if it means repeating yourself on a number of occasions this weekend, you can come through in the end. What a good day this would be to go out shopping, or to find something in the wardrobe you had forgotten you even owned.

10 SUNDAY ☿ *Moon Age Day 4 Moon Sign Taurus*

It could be that social and romantic offers are going very much your way right now. You tend to be in the good books of most people, especially one or two who appear very attractive when viewed from your side of the fence. Curb a tendency to be too outspoken, especially about matters you don't understand at all.

11 MONDAY ☿ *Moon Age Day 5 Moon Sign Taurus*

A demanding and high-energy period kicks off the start of this new working week. Filled with vitality and simply raring to get stuck in, there is nobody around who could possibly hold you back. You look and feel good, which is half the reason you impress almost everyone you meet.

12 TUESDAY ☿ *Moon Age Day 6 Moon Sign Taurus*

You find yourself running around frantically, trying to get things done that should have been completed before. In all probability, you only have yourself to blame and you know it. Nevertheless, you remain generally good-natured and friendly. Virgo is capable of great charm right now and people will remember.

13 WEDNESDAY ☿ *Moon Age Day 7 Moon Sign Gemini*

You look out for the help of those you know can be of assistance today, especially people who are expert in their own particular field. You are not lacking in confidence, though you do recognise that we can't all be good at everything. Practical jobs around the home are one area in which you might elicit support.

14 THURSDAY ☿ *Moon Age Day 8 Moon Sign Gemini*

Discussions, particularly with loved ones, can be much more important than you might have previously thought. In one or two respects, you feel that you lack courage at present. The fact that you carry on, even though you might be nervous about doing so, proves that you are actually brave.

15 FRIDAY ☿ *Moon Age Day 9* *Moon Sign Cancer*

Maybe you should sit back and take a look at your life for an hour or two today. It isn't that anything is going wrong, merely that all sorts of new opportunities wait around the corner and you won't want to miss any of them. By looking and planning now, you make such an eventuality far less likely.

16 SATURDAY ☿ *Moon Age Day 10* *Moon Sign Cancer*

What a great time this is for teamwork matters and for getting together with people who think in more or less the same way that you do. All work and no play makes Virgo a dull zodiac sign, so do make sure you are able to socialise and to chew the fat over matters that are not remotely important but still interesting.

17 SUNDAY ☿ *Moon Age Day 11* *Moon Sign Cancer*

Unexpected professional demands might appear, even though this is Sunday. If you work at the weekend you can turn these to your advantage because it is quite obvious you are being carefully watched. Don't be too quick to take offence at the offhand remarks of people who really do not mean any harm.

18 MONDAY ☿ *Moon Age Day 12* *Moon Sign Leo*

Lots of energy goes into getting what you want today. Professionally speaking this is likely to be a hard working period, but it does offer all manner of advantages that you probably did not expect. A breakthrough of some sort is indicated, possibly regarding a matter that has given you problems before.

19 TUESDAY ☿ *Moon Age Day 13* *Moon Sign Leo*

Most problem solving today is merely a matter of using your very strong intuition. Some people you come across will be quick to take offence, though this is not a stumbling block as far as you are concerned. The fact is that you are in a good frame of mind and will be taking life in your stride.

20 WEDNESDAY ☿   *Moon Age Day 14*   *Moon Sign Virgo*

Acting on impulse is part of what the lunar high inspires you to do. Under most circumstances today you simply go for what you want and manage to obtain it. It looks as though you are likely to be more dominant, though not in a way that could upset anyone else in your vicinity.

21 THURSDAY ☿   *Moon Age Day 15*   *Moon Sign Virgo*

Up early and keen to meet life head on, the lunar high inspires you to be determined regarding plans that have been in your mind for some time. Your confidence should not be lacking and even personal relationships prove to be an area in which you are able to bring people round to your point of view.

22 FRIDAY ☿   *Moon Age Day 16*   *Moon Sign Libra*

Don't take on too many commitments today. You have been pushing forward progressively for a number of days and probably need to take stock. Not everyone is around at quite the time you would wish and you might even have to show a degree of patience regarding family members or specific friends.

23 SATURDAY ☿   *Moon Age Day 17*   *Moon Sign Libra*

The weekend finds you inclined to either start or to continue pointless arguments, something you ought to avoid at all cost. Having something crucial to say is all well and good but you won't get far if you begin to bulldoze your ideas. Virgo can be very stubborn, but if you recognise this, you can also counter it.

24 SUNDAY ☿   *Moon Age Day 18*   *Moon Sign Scorpio*

Romantic encounters prove to be both eventful and rewarding, even though you might not be expecting much from them at this time. A whole succession of situations could take you more or less by surprise and you really do need to keep an open mind in order to get the very best out of the day.

25 MONDAY ☿ *Moon Age Day 19* *Moon Sign Scorpio*

At work the pace of life could be quite slow, leading you to believe that you are not making much in the way of advancement. In reality, this probably isn't the case at all. Keep an open mind about the way family members are behaving and be prepared for a good old-fashioned heart-to-heart if necessary.

26 TUESDAY ☿ *Moon Age Day 20* *Moon Sign Sagittarius*

Be careful that others don't misconstrue what you are saying today. If you suspect that this is the case, you may have to explain yourself all over again. This could be a fruitful financial period and one during which you can afford to take the odd chance. Gambles are always calculated where you are concerned.

27 WEDNESDAY ☿ *Moon Age Day 21* *Moon Sign Sagittarius*

Things quieten a little, but only if you allow life to take its own course. A proactive response works best right now, allowing you to get ahead in ways you may not have previously suspected. Surprises are the order of the day but won't appear at all unless you take this necessary hands-on approach.

28 THURSDAY ☿ *Moon Age Day 22* *Moon Sign Capricorn*

You could feel as though a personal issue of some sort is left up in the air right now, though the situation is really in your own hands. Active and enterprising, you get more into the swing of things as the day advances. This would not be the best time for outrageous risks of any sort.

29 FRIDAY *Moon Age Day 23* *Moon Sign Capricorn*

The more contemplative you are today, the greater is the chance that you will come to the right conclusion, in the end, especially about family matters. Work on and off if you can and don't tire yourself or difficulties could follow later. You may require a change of scenery, which is possible to get by the evening if not before.

30 SATURDAY   *Moon Age Day 24   Moon Sign Capricorn*

You might feel just a little irritation when it comes to your dealings with others and you should be careful not to offend anyone unintentionally. Try to make yourself as comfortable as possible this weekend because the luxury-loving side of your nature is very definitely to the fore.

31 SUNDAY   *Moon Age Day 25   Moon Sign Aquarius*

A sure-footed attitude and approach to all situations works best for this weekend. This is nothing at all unusual for you and may even be quite run of the mill. Although this may not turn out to be the most exciting Sunday you have ever lived through, it does have its strong points, particularly in a romantic relationship.

April

2019

1 MONDAY

Moon Age Day 26   Moon Sign Aquarius

In terms of communications at least, this is likely to be a hectic but enjoyable sort of day. You can afford to back your hunches to a great extent and you won't be holding back when it comes to ideas. Friends ought to prove very helpful and can offer some exciting alternatives on those occasions when life gets dull.

2 TUESDAY

Moon Age Day 27   Moon Sign Pisces

Unexpected obstacles may come along today, thanks to the lunar low. However, you are able to make the best of them and if you rely on people you know to have natural good luck, you can overcome some difficulties. On a personal level, this is a day that ought to prove both interesting and stimulating.

3 WEDNESDAY

Moon Age Day 28   Moon Sign Pisces

Your progress today is no more than modest, but you should still be interested in life generally. The needs of others could be uppermost in your mind and some headway can be made with regard to wayward relatives. Friends may be less inspirational today and might be looking for your support.

4 THURSDAY

Moon Age Day 29   Moon Sign Pisces

This is hardly the best time to be relying greatly on others, particularly people who have let you down badly in the past. If you feel like spreading the load today, it ought to be possible. Alternatively you might prefer to work alone but get difficult jobs out of the way as early in the day as possible.

5 FRIDAY
Moon Age Day 0   Moon Sign Aries

If you need a change from your everyday routines, the end of this working week could offer all the incentive you need. Keep active and don't allow yourself to vegetate. It is only a matter of time before new and stimulating situations begin, though today is unlikely to be bristling with them.

6 SATURDAY
Moon Age Day 1   Moon Sign Aries

Certain situations may seem fairly chaotic today, particularly in terms of necessary communication with others. Actually, you will probably be far better off spending some time alone and relying on your own intuition. Be cautious around get-rich-quick-schemes. If they look too good to be true, they probably are.

7 SUNDAY
Moon Age Day 2   Moon Sign Taurus

The actions of a loved one allow you to look at life in a slightly different way and could offer room for a sort of optimism that hasn't been around in the very recent past. You have managed to keep some sort of smile on your face over the last few days but there is more than a chance it is absolutely genuine today.

8 MONDAY
Moon Age Day 3   Moon Sign Taurus

Although there isn't too much coming along today to bolster your ego, you may be happy enough in the company of people who sing your praises most of the time. It might just be that you have been ignoring the attentions of someone who definitely does have your best interests at heart and who is willing to show it.

9 TUESDAY
Moon Age Day 4   Moon Sign Gemini

It's time to enjoy the fruits of some of your recent efforts. Financially speaking you could be rather better off than you have been expecting and the world looks more exciting than for some days past. You have the confidence you need to do exactly what you want. All in all, you should be looking and feeling good.

10 WEDNESDAY *Moon Age Day 5* *Moon Sign Gemini*

You are unlikely to have the time for personal indulgences today and will be tied up with one issue or another most of the time. If you can break away, do your best to foster some personal desire or aspiration. The more you feel you are moving forward, the greater is the incentive for a positive period.

11 THURSDAY *Moon Age Day 6* *Moon Sign Gemini*

A rather pressing domestic matter could arise today. Take it in your stride and don't necessarily think that you have to find answers here and now. There are certain issues that would be best left alone for the moment, leaving you to have fun and to look at life in a much broader manner.

12 FRIDAY *Moon Age Day 7* *Moon Sign Cancer*

It does appear that material issues are uppermost in your mind at present and you need to face some of these head-on and early in the day. At work, you are positive and aspiring, though it is in terms of love and romance that you tend to have the best of all worlds today. People simply want to love you and to be kind.

13 SATURDAY *Moon Age Day 8* *Moon Sign Cancer*

Achieving a good balance between self-interest and the need others have of you will not be too difficult today. Although you are still very committed to change, you can also see just how important it would be to think carefully before you act. A very sensible Virgoan is what the world registers today.

14 SUNDAY *Moon Age Day 9* *Moon Sign Leo*

Sunday offers positive trends, but you may find it hard to deal with any problems involving logic. You have plenty of get-up-and-go and so would probably get the most fun this weekend from doing something out of doors. Being with family members is certainly no hardship at this time.

15 MONDAY   *Moon Age Day 10   Moon Sign Leo*

You are so preoccupied with personal issues today that you fail to see the wood for the trees in a practical sense. In any situation, it is very important to keep your eye on the ball. This probably isn't the best time of the month to make any major financial changes in any case. Stick with the status quo.

16 TUESDAY   *Moon Age Day 11   Moon Sign Virgo*

In financial affairs you may be open to discussion today, a fact that can pay dividends later on. Affairs of the heart should be progressing in a satisfactory manner, and as the day advances, the benefits of the lunar high show themselves more and more. Keep a high profile in social situations.

17 WEDNESDAY   *Moon Age Day 12   Moon Sign Virgo*

This is a good time to exploit a potentially lucky period. Success now doesn't really depend on risk, but you will be inclined to back your own hunches and to make it plan to others that you know your own business best. Confident and quite dynamic, the world is going to take notice of you now.

18 THURSDAY   *Moon Age Day 13   Moon Sign Libra*

Clearer communication is called for today because it would be very easy for your comments to be misconstrued by others. Keep confidences that others trust in you, and take a lot of care in the way you approach particularly sensitive types. Make sure you also get some exercise at some stage today.

19 FRIDAY   *Moon Age Day 14   Moon Sign Libra*

This is day on which you can be very constructive and during which you can come to a number of conclusions that you might not have reached in the recent past. Arguing your point of view is unlikely to get you into trouble because others will accept that you are entitled to a different opinion from theirs.

20 SATURDAY   *Moon Age Day 15   Moon Sign Scorpio*

You should focus on the short-term as far as your plans are concerned. It looks as though you will have little or no difficulty in keeping up with anything that is going on in your vicinity. This is a period during which your stubborn side turns out to be a distinct advantage as it will mean that you won't give in under any circumstances.

21 SUNDAY   *Moon Age Day 16   Moon Sign Scorpio*

Input and information relating to your current dreams and schemes comes in from every conceivable direction at this time. There are people around who prove to be extremely interesting and who will want to be on your side. Friendships can be made around now and old pals come back to the fore.

22 MONDAY   *Moon Age Day 17   Moon Sign Sagittarius*

Socially speaking, you may be the centre of attention. This is not always an ideal situation for you but at the moment it is unlikely to bother you in the slightest. Don't be prepared to make too many compromises regarding issues about which you feel very strongly. You might upset someone but not much.

23 TUESDAY   *Moon Age Day 18   Moon Sign Sagittarius*

Trends indicate that events from the past could replay themselves in stark terms today. Some of this should be easy to deal with, but some could be a concern. Your confidence in the people you love grows stronger as someone close to you takes action above and beyond the call of duty.

24 WEDNESDAY   *Moon Age Day 19   Moon Sign Capricorn*

Partnerships enhance your love of life and you find even people coming new to your scene are easy to get along with. Younger Virgoans could be making friends around now who will be present for years to come. Give yourself a big pat on the back in light of a job you know has been well done.

25 THURSDAY *Moon Age Day 20 Moon Sign Capricorn*

The focus is now on personal and financial matters, perhaps even to the extent that anything else is peripheral. Your ability to concentrate is noteworthy, but don't forget there is a big, wide world out there and you can't ignore it. Travel is likely for some Virgoans, especially if it is related to work.

26 FRIDAY *Moon Age Day 21 Moon Sign Capricorn*

Trends suggest that you will be busily rushing about today, particularly at work. Amongst the frenetic activity don't forget to pay some attention to personal matters which, in truth, should be your number one concern. You may gain by making a new start.

27 SATURDAY *Moon Age Day 22 Moon Sign Aquarius*

Single Virgos have a better than ever chance of making a new start in the area of personal relationships now, whilst those in more settled relationships will be pepping things up somehow. The weekend is good for any sort of activity, but especially those taking place in the great outdoors.

28 SUNDAY *Moon Age Day 23 Moon Sign Aquarius*

There is a real sense of harmony about now, and much of it comes directly from you. If you have been working hard on a new project for a while you should now be noticing a degree of success. Every dog has his or her day and Virgo can expect a payback for concentrated effort across the last few months.

29 MONDAY *Moon Age Day 24 Moon Sign Pisces*

Progress in practical matters now slows down, as the lunar low takes the wind out of your sails. This does not mean you fail to achieve anything, merely that you need to go at things slowly and with great concentration. One job done well is worth a hundred that don't get the attention they truly deserve.

30 TUESDAY

Moon Age Day 25   Moon Sign Pisces

There are likely to be a few disappointments today but none of them will be of any real importance. The lunar low is inclined to take the edge off enjoyment, at least until later in the day. It would be best not to expect too much and to keep wishes modest. In the evening you will probably give yourself to family matters.

May

2019

1 WEDNESDAY

Moon Age Day 26   Moon Sign Pisces

Change and diversity are the legacies of today's planetary influences. A stay-at-home routine sort of mid week probably won't suit you at all. On the contrary, you prefer to be out and about, mixing with the people you like to be with. By the evening, you can really put your social hat on.

2 THURSDAY

Moon Age Day 27   Moon Sign Aries

If anything, the pace of everyday life gets swifter, leaving you little time today to watch the flowers grow. However, these are not trends that life imposes on you but rather ones you actively encourage yourself. When practical matters do come along it might be hard now to concentrate on the job at hand.

3 FRIDAY

Moon Age Day 28   Moon Sign Aries

Certain astrological trends are still working well on your behalf and they offer you the chance to make progress in areas of life that could have been ignored of late. Comfort and security, never far from the Virgo mind under present circumstances also make an appearance, particularly later in the day. Look out for some solid financial possibilities.

4 SATURDAY

Moon Age Day 0   Moon Sign Taurus

It is quite clear today that you cannot please all of the people, all of the time. Instead of trying to do so, stick to those people with whom you have most in common. Contentious issues should be left on the shelf and dealt with at a later date – in fact as late as possible.

5 SUNDAY
Moon Age Day 1   Moon Sign Taurus

There ought to be plenty of good things happening around you, even though you might feel that not all that many are happening to you. Be patient because other people have the right to make progress too and today is a time when you are in a particularly good position to help them out. Generosity on your part brings its own rewards.

6 MONDAY
Moon Age Day 2   Moon Sign Taurus

Your quick-fire mind is likely to be on display today, as others admire your sharp logic. With a ready wit and an ability to turn heads, you move progressively towards your objectives now. There are hints that romance could be on the cards, particularly if you make some extra effort.

7 TUESDAY
Moon Age Day 3   Moon Sign Gemini

Along comes an influence that allows you to attract the good things in life. Although you won't be able to make everything happen in quite the way you would wish, there are gains to be made by simply being in the right place at the right time. To ensure this is possible, simply turn your intuition up to full.

8 WEDNESDAY
Moon Age Day 4   Moon Sign Gemini

There are opportunities to get ahead in practical matters today but whether or not you take them remains to be seen. You may be preoccupied with your social life and also concerned to put extra effort into relationships. It is clear that you cannot achieve every objective so you are right to pace yourself.

9 THURSDAY
Moon Age Day 5   Moon Sign Cancer

It may well benefit you to be a bit pushier now than you sometimes are. Not everyone is doing what they can to improve situations around you and it may be up to you to put things back on track. This will be particularly true if you are a working Virgo with specific and important responsibilities.

10 FRIDAY   *Moon Age Day 6   Moon Sign Cancer*

Your personal associations with others show just how strong your influence now is. Not only do people want to listen to what you have to say, they almost instinctively follow your lead. Routines are not acceptable to you today, instead you want to be instinctive and to do what comes naturally moment-by-moment.

11 SATURDAY   *Moon Age Day 7   Moon Sign Leo*

Striking personal successes become possible today, as the Moon moves into your zodiac sign. Go for what you want with all guns blazing, but don't upset anyone else on the way. Your approach is now very progressive and you should be filled with good ideas that are also practical ones.

12 SUNDAY   *Moon Age Day 8   Moon Sign Leo*

This would be an excellent time to tackle people who definitely have influence over your life. You could be taking on new projects and generally finding ways to be more successful and, of course, comfortable. You are bright and alert, and this in turn makes you extremely popular.

13 MONDAY   *Moon Age Day 9   Moon Sign Virgo*

Certain discussions in the wider world could have an argumentative side to them, something you will probably want to avoid. Although you wish to put your point of view across, there isn't much point in making enemies on the way. A gentler approach works better, so defuse situations when you can.

14 TUESDAY   *Moon Age Day 10   Moon Sign Virgo*

Present trends do not indicate that this is the best time to flex your intellect. Some of your decision-making is a little rusty and you will have to spend time thinking things through. Keep an open mind about changes in and around your home, perhaps leaving some of them until later.

15 WEDNESDAY   *Moon Age Day 11   Moon Sign Libra*

You ought to be able to latch on to better financial trends that come along any time now. This is not an area of life that you will be thinking about exclusively, but it does need attention. Friends may prove to be demanding, but what they give back is worth any amount of effort on your part today.

16 THURSDAY   *Moon Age Day 12   Moon Sign Libra*

Today could see specific financial or professional gains coming your way and would be an ideal time to start new projects, particularly at work. When the responsibilities are out of the way, you should think about having fun. It's a mix and match sort of day, with periods of high activity and other times when you can relax.

17 FRIDAY   *Moon Age Day 13   Moon Sign Scorpio*

Power challenges are likely today, but you have a unique way of dealing with them. Flying off the handle certainly isn't your way right now and wouldn't work too well in any case. Your present gentle and considered approach is all you need.

18 SATURDAY   *Moon Age Day 14   Moon Sign Scorpio*

Energy wise, you achieve a sort of peak today and can also make gains as a result of the very real efforts of those around you. If there is a particular job that needs doing, get it out of the way early in the day, leaving yourself with more time later for whatever takes your personal fancy.

19 SUNDAY   *Moon Age Day 15   Moon Sign Scorpio*

Look out for a little extra good fortune today, which might bring some unexpected cash into your pocket. There is a penchant on your part right now for the odd or the unusual. At the same time, you could find yourself looking back at situations from quite a long time ago.

20 MONDAY *Moon Age Day 16 Moon Sign Sagittarius*

This may turn out to be one of the best social times of the month and maybe of the year. Stay out there in the social limelight and be prepared to take the lead when others indicate you should do so. You are about to realise just how popular and also how capable your sign of Virgo can be.

21 TUESDAY *Moon Age Day 17 Moon Sign Sagittarius*

This should be an enjoyable time as far as your love life is concerned. You seem to be particularly charming at the moment and can certainly turn heads. Avoid unnecessary routines and concentrate on those matters you know to be of supreme importance. Keep a sense of proportion over professional matters.

22 WEDNESDAY *Moon Age Day 18 Moon Sign Capricorn*

In a monetary sense you are now in a position to get ahead. This probably has to do with your efforts over the last few months and has not come from nowhere. Stand up for someone who you think is going through a bad time and argue their corner with all the tenacity of which your zodiac sign is capable.

23 THURSDAY *Moon Age Day 19 Moon Sign Capricorn*

Every day events keep you pretty much on the move, so you can forget any idea that today might be restful. You rush about from one task to another but since your energy level is high, this won't be a problem. In amongst all you take on, social trends are good and you will find time to mix freely.

24 FRIDAY *Moon Age Day 20 Moon Sign Aquarius*

Now you are likely to disagree openly with people whose attitudes you don't care for. It is often the case that Virgo keeps its counsel, but present trends show that you are inclined to speak out. Look for some real personalities entering your life and make the most of their refreshing presence.

25 SATURDAY
Moon Age Day 21   Moon Sign Aquarius

Avenues of communication are wide open. If you want to get your message across, now is the time to do so. You remain essentially reasonable in your attitude and tend to make friends wherever you go. Push hard towards a chosen objective and don't allow those who are just naturally grumpy to get in your way.

26 SUNDAY
Moon Age Day 22   Moon Sign Aquarius

The emphasis is now on communication and it ought to be obvious from the start of the day that your chatty side is on display. With boundless energy there is very little to stand in your way. Your creative potential is also strong and funds all manner of new activities.

27 MONDAY
Moon Age Day 23   Moon Sign Pisces

The lunar low now brings a quieter phase and might make it difficult for you to register any particular progress just now. Instead of swimming against the stream, it would be better to take life steadily now. There are plenty of people around who will be of assistance if you want them to be.

28 TUESDAY
Moon Age Day 24   Moon Sign Pisces

Avoid disappointments by not allowing yourself to get into positions that could prove awkward. There might be periods of relative silence today, but if so they tend to be chosen, rather than thrust upon you. Consideration for others is usually high up in your priorities and there is no reason to believe that today will be any different.

29 WEDNESDAY
Moon Age Day 25   Moon Sign Aries

There may be some problems arising now from money, or perhaps the lack of it. This is not a situation that is going to stop you in your tracks. On the contrary, it inspires in you that fantastic ability of Virgo to make do and mend. Ingenious and positive, you can make a tremendous impression on the world.

30 THURSDAY   *Moon Age Day 26   Moon Sign Aries*

The tide turns and you suddenly have less time to spend with others, if only because you are so busy keeping up with the practical requirements of life. There are some unusual circumstances today, particularly a series of coincidences. These can be unsettling but turn to your advantage.

31 FRIDAY   *Moon Age Day 27   Moon Sign Aries*

You will both work and play hard at this time, so yet another day is likely to be eventful and even riotous. Be careful because you are not indestructible. There are gains to be made from a financial point of view, and some of them may come from unexpected directions. Love comes knocking around now.

2019

1 SATURDAY
Moon Age Day 28   Moon Sign Taurus

This is a day during which you should see things happening on the material plane. Try to spend money wisely, even if there is more cash coming in today than usual. In other areas, not everyone appears to understand your point of view, particularly regarding personal matters, but you should be able to talk them round.

2 SUNDAY
Moon Age Day 29   Moon Sign Taurus

Your powers of communication especially are in the ascendant today and you seem to have what it takes to get your message across to others. If there is a particularly big task before you, the best approach today may be to nibble away at the edges of it or maybe to seek the help of a good friend.

3 MONDAY
Moon Age Day 0   Moon Sign Gemini

Though you might feel yourself more than ready to take a break, the considerable responsibilities you face at present make this less than likely. Conforming to expectations won't be all that easy right now and you would be better off allowing a degree of originality to enter your reasoning today.

4 TUESDAY
Moon Age Day 1   Moon Sign Gemini

There may be some tensions in everyday matters that need to be dealt with fairly early in the day. However, don't allow these to distract you from the real job at hand, which is to promote yourself in a public forum. People really do want to hear what you have to say and you are hardly shy right now.

5 WEDNESDAY   *Moon Age Day 2   Moon Sign Cancer*

Although you could be in two minds regarding practical decisions, in the end your practical common sense can tell you what to do. Do you take the advice of others or simply forge ahead under your own steam? For once, the answer isn't in the stars but is solely dictated by logic at this time.

6 THURSDAY   *Moon Age Day 3   Moon Sign Cancer*

It is likely that your financial powers are still looking reasonably good, even if you have to stretch cash somewhat today. Don't spend lavishly on items you don't really need and do be prepared to keep an open mind about bargains. Friends are on your side, particularly in little disputes that are arising at work.

7 FRIDAY   *Moon Age Day 4   Moon Sign Leo*

Relationships now prove more rewarding than they might have seemed on one or two occasions recently. Close to home there are people who display their goodwill and who actively want to offer you some sort of support. This may not be needed but it would be churlish to turn the people in question away.

8 SATURDAY   *Moon Age Day 5   Moon Sign Leo*

Though your practical capabilities are excellent at the moment, the part of your mind that governs how you arrange matters isn't quite as well honed. It might be necessary to check things with other people and even to follow their lead in some matters. This weekend would be excellent for shopping and for meeting up with friends in an informal way.

9 SUNDAY   *Moon Age Day 6   Moon Sign Virgo*

The lunar high now brings acceleration to the pace of your life and makes this a rather less than relaxing summer Sunday. You have masses to keep you occupied and all the energy necessary to deal with what comes along. Friendship is particularly well accented later in the day.

10 MONDAY
Moon Age Day 7   Moon Sign Virgo

The start of this new working week ought to prove to be an excellent time to take the odd chance and to stamp your own particular brand of authority on your life. Few people would want to stand in your way at this time and you can afford to back your hunches, probably to the hilt.

11 TUESDAY
Moon Age Day 8   Moon Sign Virgo

Today finds you dealing with frayed tempers, though almost certainly not your own. It is possible to get through far more work today than you could possibly have expected, leaving you with social moments that are snatched but very important. Hand out some congratulations in the family.

12 WEDNESDAY
Moon Age Day 9   Moon Sign Libra

This is a good period on the whole for broadening your horizons and for seeking new things to do. The day can be stimulating and even exciting in a way you had not expected. You make a strong contribution to family events but should also be able to find times to be extremely supportive of your partner or a friend.

13 THURSDAY
Moon Age Day 10   Moon Sign Libra

Intellectual exchanges take place today and offer you the chance to sharpen your intellect in a way that hasn't been possible for quite some time. Try to stay away from artificial stimulants of any sort right now. Your brain is managing to produce enough stimulating chemicals of its own.

14 FRIDAY
Moon Age Day 11   Moon Sign Scorpio

You may have to be rather cautious when approaching others because there are some very sensitive types around at the moment. Routines can get on your nerves today and it is quite plain to see that you want to break the bounds of convention in as many ways as you can. That's fine but others may not agree.

15 SATURDAY   *Moon Age Day 12   Moon Sign Scorpio*

This could be a good time to put financial plans into action, most likely in conjunction with either business or personal partners. As far as romance is concerned, you should be looking out today for someone who is clearly making overtures. Whether you are interested or not remains to be seen, but you should be flattered.

16 SUNDAY   *Moon Age Day 13   Moon Sign Sagittarius*

Personal finance could be a slight cause for concern and it is probable that you are going to have to rein in your spending somewhat. Don't be too quick to take offence if a friend says the wrong thing but ask for a fuller explanation. You can be just a little quick off the mark around this time.

17 MONDAY   *Moon Age Day 14   Moon Sign Sagittarius*

There are many new possibilities around at the start of this week. It seems almost certain that you are still on top form and that you will be making the most of what the day has to offer. In particular you should find there are opportunities to take journeys and to show someone special how you feel.

18 TUESDAY   *Moon Age Day 15   Moon Sign Capricorn*

Don't miss out on anything important that is happening in or around your personal world at the moment. During this whole week you will be inclined to keep your eyes open, but are less likely to be paying full attention today. This might be a pity because it really counts at present.

19 WEDNESDAY   *Moon Age Day 16   Moon Sign Capricorn*

There could be some sort of return to the past now, even if this only takes place inside your head. It may not be easy to be totally comfortable today, especially since this is the first day for some time during which you have moments to spare. The problem is going to be working out how to use them.

20 THURSDAY   *Moon Age Day 17*   *Moon Sign Capricorn*

You will be ready to exchange ideas with just about anyone today and won't be afraid to offer your considered opinion. Someone is very special to you right now, probably because of favours they have done on your behalf. Life might not always be ideal at the moment, but it is stimulating.

21 FRIDAY   *Moon Age Day 18*   *Moon Sign Aquarius*

You may well have your work cut out today trying to keep on top of material problems, which is why it would be very sensible to call upon the help and advice of people who are genuinely in the know. Rules are easy to follow, but more difficult for family members.

22 SATURDAY   *Moon Age Day 19*   *Moon Sign Aquarius*

Your sympathies are easily roused today, which is why you make such a good friend and will be so willing to put yourself out for others. Don't become too soft, however, because you could find yourself going to great trouble to support those who have no intention of helping themselves.

23 SUNDAY   *Moon Age Day 20*   *Moon Sign Pisces*

Along comes a time to seek out some intellectual stimulation. What you don't need right now is to become bored by situations. Better by far to change direction at any moment today, rather than to find any task tedious. There is a restlessness about you at present that is difficult to address.

24 MONDAY   *Moon Age Day 21*   *Moon Sign Pisces*

Obstacles and hold-ups of one sort or another are clearly a fact of life at the moment and there is little you can do to address or alter them. The lunar low isn't around long, but it has made you rather lethargic and less inclined to concentrate. Simply understand what is going on astrologically and all will come right.

25 TUESDAY   *Moon Age Day 22   Moon Sign Pisces*

Beware of certain emotional drives at the moment that might lead you off a sensible path and towards difficulties. In your romantic life there is a danger that you could be too intense. Perhaps you are looking for something that doesn't exist or else deluding yourself in some other way. Try to back off and take things at face value.

26 WEDNESDAY   *Moon Age Day 23   Moon Sign Aries*

The greater the range of interests you take on at the moment, the better you will enjoy life. You don't have to carry all your ideas into the future but taking them out of the drawer of your mind for a good examination at least allows you to decide what would be worth more effort in the longer-term.

27 THURSDAY   *Moon Age Day 24   Moon Sign Aries*

The deeper and more secret aspects of your personality are now under scrutiny, and not just by you. Expect some very leading questions to be coming in around this time and prepare for the fact that it might be rather difficult to answer some of them. This can be hard for Virgo which, at heart, enjoys and protects its secrecy.

28 FRIDAY   *Moon Age Day 25   Moon Sign Taurus*

People come and go all the time now and it may be difficult to keep track of them. For your own part, you might prefer to take a rest and to simply watch the flowers grow for a few hours. All work and no play is not good for anyone, a fact you are inclined to realise eventually. There are good family trends around today.

29 SATURDAY   *Moon Age Day 26   Moon Sign Taurus*

Daily encounters with others keep you abreast of what is going on in your immediate vicinity but that probably isn't quite enough for you now. You are watching the television news and scanning the newspapers in order to see what is going on the world outside your door. Virgo is very alert now.

30 SUNDAY

Moon Age Day 27   *Moon Sign Gemini*

Your potential good fortune in the finance department comes mainly through keeping your eye on the ball. The weekend can be quite useful in this regard, not least of all because you are on the receiving end of help from friends and acquaintances. Don't miss the chance of a small but fortunate speculation.

July

2019

1 MONDAY
Moon Age Day 28   Moon Sign Gemini

Career developments may need more attention at the start of this working week. It could be that you are faced with certain choices or even changes. It isn't hard for you to see your way forward at present or to make the sort of decisions that will have you feeling more secure in the weeks and months to come.

2 TUESDAY
Moon Age Day 0   Moon Sign Gemini

Although you know what you want from life, you are inclined to be easily influenced today. It is important to stick to directions you have chosen for yourself previously and not to be diverted by false promises. A special friendship really begins to blossom at this time and in your spare moments you can achieve a sort of inner peace.

3 WEDNESDAY
Moon Age Day 1   Moon Sign Cancer

There is a renewed sense of urgency where specific plans are concerned and you might feel under some sort of pressure, particularly at work. You do tend to take a rather sensible attitude to life across the board and this allows you to look rationally at issues that could have been troublesome earlier.

4 THURSDAY
Moon Age Day 2   Moon Sign Cancer

Though you are great company for others, you may not have quite the belief in your own abilities that they have in you. It might be sensible to take a look in their direction. If they trust and respect you so much, wouldn't it be sensible to listen to their opinions? You have very little to lose and much to gain.

5 FRIDAY
Moon Age Day 3   Moon Sign Leo

Keep your eyes and ears open for news and views, some of which is both surprising and interesting. The approaching weekend should bring a great deal of variety, plus a desire for fresh fields and pastures new. This is not especially unusual at this time of year and can be catered for by planning or actually taking a holiday.

6 SATURDAY
Moon Age Day 4   Moon Sign Leo

A discussion with someone very close to you can lead to decisions that could not have been taken even a few days ago. There is a strong need for you to feel secure today and that can be catered for by simply talking to the people you love and live with. Reassurance can also come from the direction of friends.

7 SUNDAY
Moon Age Day 5   Moon Sign Virgo

This is probably the best part of the month for actually getting things done. The lunar high brings greater confidence and allows you to influence others in ways that may not have been possible earlier. This is especially true today with regard to family members, friends and, of course, your partner.

8 MONDAY
☿ *Moon Age Day 6   Moon Sign Virgo*

You want to cram as much in as you can at this time, but you also have to bear in mind that under present planetary trends social possibilities are legion. Not to worry. You know how to pace yourself and in any case, the level of energy you display right now appears to be going well off the scale.

9 TUESDAY
☿ *Moon Age Day 7   Moon Sign Libra*

Romance and social matters keep you well at the forefront of activities today. While it is still early in the week, you may be longing for the weekend already so that you can maximise your potential in this area. If you are feeling out of sorts later in the day, simply rely on the support that proves to be a natural part of your present, elevated, popularity.

10 WEDNESDAY ☿   *Moon Age Day 8   Moon Sign Libra*

Family matters and the domestic scene is your preferred resort now. It's true that you can get on well at work, but the amount of effort you have to put in is tremendous. If you have the time today get round to listening to some music, maybe something you have been meaning to give your attention to for a while.

11 THURSDAY ☿   *Moon Age Day 9   Moon Sign Scorpio*

Trips down memory lane are fine, but they don't butter any bread. It is in the world of practicalities that you tend to find yourself today and there are many issues that have to be addressed. Although you remain fairly busy, there should also be more than enough time to find ways in which you can have fun.

12 FRIDAY ☿   *Moon Age Day 10   Moon Sign Scorpio*

You continue to take life in your stride and are unlikely to be fazed by much on what proves to be a fairly sensible sort of day for Virgo. Sensible is fine, but it doesn't create excitement, and you need some of that too. Try not to be willing to settle for second best, but push forward progressively.

13 SATURDAY ☿ *Moon Age Day 11   Moon Sign Sagittarius*

Professional and career-related matters could move up a notch now, even though the weekend has arrived. You might be coming to the end of a task or phase that in some ways you will be happy to leave behind. This may not be the most satisfying of days, but it does appear to bring a good deal of inner contentment.

14 SUNDAY ☿ *Moon Age Day 12   Moon Sign Sagittarius*

Watch out for strained relationships, even if you have not been causing the problems yourself. There are times when it is necessary to stand back and look at particular issues. You could find today to be such a period. Rules and regulations could easily get on your nerves today, so try to stay clear of them.

15 MONDAY ☿ *Moon Age Day 13* *Moon Sign Capricorn*

You feel much easier now about making your way in the world of work. You are fairly fortunate at present because there are plenty of people around who are willing to lend a helping hand when you need it the most. However, not every situation can be addressed today and some patience is necessary.

16 TUESDAY ☿ *Moon Age Day 14* *Moon Sign Capricorn*

This would be a wonderful period for relaxing at home, though you might find there is a wealth of things to get done before this proves to be possible. Domestic comfort really appeals at the moment and it looks as though the more progressive qualities of Virgo are taking a holiday.

17 WEDNESDAY ☿ *Moon Age Day 15* *Moon Sign Capricorn*

High spirits and a positive attitude should be prevailing today, making this an excellent time to try out new skills. At work, people are relying on you and it is certain you will come up with the goods when it proves important to do so. The attitude of some friends could be puzzling.

18 THURSDAY ☿ *Moon Age Day 16* *Moon Sign Aquarius*

Encounters with people you haven't seen for some time could be just what the doctor ordered on this Thursday. Even very early in the day your mind is working clearly and it isn't at all difficult to see through the mist of uncertainty that has been hanging around for a while.

19 FRIDAY ☿ *Moon Age Day 17* *Moon Sign Aquarius*

You could find that much of today passes at a rapid pace. Someone you haven't seen for quite some time could make a return to your life. Thoughts of travel could also be occupying your mind, perhaps making it difficult to concentrate on the more mundane aspects of life that are inevitable right now.

20 SATURDAY ☿ *Moon Age Day 18   Moon Sign Pisces*

Right now the lunar low is around. True, it doesn't have the bearing on Virgo that it does on some zodiac signs, but it can take the wind out of your sails to a certain extent. Adopt a matter of fact attitude and simply enjoy the peace and quiet that a summer Saturday can offer. Try to relax if you can.

21 SUNDAY ☿ *Moon Age Day 19   Moon Sign Pisces*

A certain degree of diplomacy is called for at this time, maybe during a period when you are really not in the best frame of mind to offer it. Try to slow things down and take life steadily. There is nothing to be gained at all today from rushing your fences. You have tremendous staying power but need to get some rest too.

22 MONDAY ☿ *Moon Age Day 20   Moon Sign Pisces*

You need to feel busy and useful but there is far more to life than the short-term achievements you make today, beneficial as these are. Medium and longer-term planning is important, making sure that you take on board the help and advice of family members and friends who are simply bursting to lend a hand.

23 TUESDAY ☿ *Moon Age Day 21   Moon Sign Aries*

You should find that talks or simple encounters today could be very stimulating. Life is generally rewarding and certainly more interesting than seems to have been the case for the last week or so. The attitude of one or two friends might be puzzling but it also intrigues you and makes you want to investigate further.

24 WEDNESDAY ☿ *Moon Age Day 22   Moon Sign Aries*

Some emotional issues rise to the surface at the moment, bringing you to a realisation that you need to address them. Facing problems, even small ones, head-on, is something you try to avoid doing, but in the end you will have little choice. Someone you know well can be of tremendous help.

25 THURSDAY ☿ *Moon Age Day 23* *Moon Sign Taurus*

Your judgement is now especially good and represents your single best quality for the moment. Not all attitudes that come your way are of equal merit and you need to be able to sort out the wheat from the chaff. Conforming to expectations in a personal sense could provide the odd problem so think carefully.

26 FRIDAY ☿ *Moon Age Day 24* *Moon Sign Taurus*

There is a strong influence today on home and family matters. Although it is clear that you remain busy in other ways, it is towards your domain and the people in it that your mind is inclined to turn. Avoid getting too tied up with technical details that can easily be sorted out later.

27 SATURDAY ☿ *Moon Age Day 25* *Moon Sign Taurus*

You could benefit from a brief withdrawal phase and would be quite happy doing something that simply suits you. Of course, there are still responsibilities to be dealt with and you will probably want to get these out of the way as early in the day as you can manage. Make it your business to remove doubt from a relative's mind if necessary.

28 SUNDAY ☿ *Moon Age Day 26* *Moon Sign Gemini*

You should be able to talk anyone into just about anything you wish at the moment. Your powers of communication are especially good and your intellect is razor sharp. The attitude of your partner might be puzzling until you stop to think about things fully. People from the past enter your life again around now.

29 MONDAY ☿ *Moon Age Day 27* *Moon Sign Gemini*

Your energy is still noteworthy and represents your best chance of getting ahead at present. Confidence remains high and feeds you with a new type of inspiration. Someone who is going to be very important to your future might make an appearance in your life around now, so keep your eyes open.

30 TUESDAY ☿ *Moon Age Day 28 Moon Sign Cancer*

A little more care and diplomacy is necessary when you are handling certain matters today, especially those related to friends. It would be very easy to give offence without meaning to do so. Explain yourself fully at every opportunity and don't allow interruptions to get in the way of common civility.

31 WEDNESDAY ☿ *Moon Age Day 0 Moon Sign Cancer*

You can be the main attraction in social groups at this stage of the working week. Allying personal matters to your job, you find it quite easy to turn heads and should be the centre of attention most of the time. Stay away from pointless arguments and concentrate on having a good time when possible.

August

2019

1 THURSDAY
Moon Age Day 1   Moon Sign Leo

Don't worry about a lack of energy as August gets started. You are very keen to make a favourable impression, particularly on someone who is especially important to your personal life. The opinions of family members will not always favour your present plans, so some swift talking is called for.

2 FRIDAY
Moon Age Day 2   Moon Sign Leo

Good communication and plenty of feedback is part of what can make today special. Stay away from mundane tasks as much as you can and stick to making a good impression. The more you mix with others, the greater will be your sense of purpose and your ability to forge new paths.

3 SATURDAY
Moon Age Day 3   Moon Sign Virgo

Now the brakes are off and you are pushing forward with much more energy and a greater chance of success. What an amazing weekend this could be. The lunar high offers you the ability to make a good impression, and also increases your desire to see fresh fields and pastures new. Don't hold back.

4 SUNDAY
Moon Age Day 4   Moon Sign Virgo

As was the case yesterday you can get your own way and make life work out more or less the way you would wish now. Give yourself a pat on the back for something you have just achieved, but don't allow the situation to go to your head. There is plenty more to do, and right now you have the energy to move mountains.

5 MONDAY
Moon Age Day 5   Moon Sign Libra

Avoid getting carried away with schemes that quite frankly don't have all that much chance of working to your advantage. There are gains to be made today, though these are not all that likely to be financial in nature. Relationships look good, as do all social and sporting efforts on your part today.

6 TUESDAY
Moon Age Day 6   Moon Sign Libra

You may decide to wind down certain activities, at least for the moment. The fact is that you are feeling a little lack-lustre today and will be happier to let someone else take the strain. Some great chances are not too far away and it is likely that you will actively want to plan ahead of them. That requires time to think.

7 WEDNESDAY
Moon Age Day 7   Moon Sign Scorpio

The art of good conversation is certainly not dead as far as you are concerned. Start today by chatting to just about anyone who will listen and be prepared to be singled out to speak on behalf of others. Your leadership skills are now being recognised, even if you don't consider you have any.

8 THURSDAY
Moon Age Day 8   Moon Sign Scorpio

It might be evident that hearth and home is the place you want to be and that you are not all that keen to be out and about too much today. This may be a good thing. Dashing around from pillar to post for days on end is not really what your zodiac sign is all about. All the same you are very purposeful when at work.

9 FRIDAY
Moon Age Day 9   Moon Sign Sagittarius

The challenge now seems to be getting yourself in the right place to do those things you feel to be important. Don't worry about possible support because that should be around as and when you need it. There are some interesting people crossing your path in the near future and a few of them will prove to be good friends.

10 SATURDAY · *Moon Age Day 10 · Moon Sign Sagittarius*

Domestic matters can get in the way of your personal freedom today, something you don't want to happen during a Saturday. Sort out any minor irritations in the family early on and then you will be free to do whatever takes your fancy. Some Virgoans see this as being a time for turning over a new leaf.

11 SUNDAY · *Moon Age Day 11 · Moon Sign Sagittarius*

It is clear that you intend to be noticed today and that isn't surprising because in one way or another you are putting on a very good show. Concentrate on the task at hand when necessary and then remain determined to have a good time later. Schedules and deadlines might be a little frustrating, though not for long.

12 MONDAY · *Moon Age Day 12 · Moon Sign Capricorn*

You may have to focus on minor tasks today because it's the little jobs that add up to successes later on. What matters most about today are the hours when you are not at work. Not only do things look particularly good on the romantic front, but you will also find yourself making a favourable impression on strangers.

13 TUESDAY · *Moon Age Day 13 · Moon Sign Capricorn*

A joint financial venture could prove to be something of a headache and you need to be careful that you have thought everything through carefully. Meanwhile, there could be events happening in the family that both please and displease you for different reasons. Striking the right balance in your relationships takes tact.

14 WEDNESDAY · *Moon Age Day 14 · Moon Sign Aquarius*

Try to get away somewhere around about this time. Even if you don't have a holiday planned, a shorter change of scene would do you the world of good. What you definitely don't need at this time of year is to be stuck indoors, with no view of nature and no gentle breeze blowing across your face.

15 THURSDAY   *Moon Age Day 15   Moon Sign Aquarius*

Stand by for a few disagreements, caused as much as anything by misunderstandings. Talk matters through carefully and freely because that is the way to avoid arguments. Although you feel quite passionate about specific matters, it might be best not to push the point home too hard. Instead, seek a peaceful day.

16 FRIDAY   *Moon Age Day 16   Moon Sign Aquarius*

A new sense of willpower is evident, so it isn't hard for you to begin some new regime if that is the way you are feeling. At the same time, you are much less likely to back away from issues that have caused you some concern in the past. You might not get through masses of work today but what you do is done well.

17 SATURDAY   *Moon Age Day 17   Moon Sign Pisces*

Energy is not plentiful this weekend and if the weather is good, you might opt for a few hours sitting in the garden or pottering around in the flower beds. Any sort of frenetic activity is likely to be out of the window and from a social point of view you should be keeping it steady and gentle.

18 SUNDAY   *Moon Age Day 18   Moon Sign Pisces*

Although it could appear right now that the grass in greener on the other side of just about any fence, this isn't the case at all. Simply plod along and enjoy the gains that those around you are making. This is your chance to recharge flagging batteries because by tomorrow you will be up to speed again.

19 MONDAY   *Moon Age Day 19   Moon Sign Aries*

With a strong sense of optimism that seems to be rewarded at every turn, you are clearly a force to be reckoned with at the moment. Friends crowd in to help you with projects that seem particularly important and you show a positive face to all manner of new incentives that begin around this time.

20 TUESDAY *Moon Age Day 20   Moon Sign Aries*

You need to set aside some quality time in order to please your nearest and dearest. This can be an action packed Tuesday but that doesn't really help if someone you care about is feeling distinctly left out of situations. Sharing yourself out isn't easy today, but it could prove to be quite necessary.

21 WEDNESDAY *Moon Age Day 21   Moon Sign Aries*

It is possible that your ideas regarding the way things should be done are a little unrealistic and once you come to recognise that you could well turn to someone wise for advice. Your attitude towards those who are having problems is very good and there isn't much doubt that the truly sensitive side of Virgo is in evidence.

22 THURSDAY *Moon Age Day 22   Moon Sign Taurus*

Although you are channelling all your energy into various pursuits today, there might be just the hint of a feeling that you are working too hard for very little gain. Maybe you need to rethink certain plans, or perhaps find out from someone else where you might be going slightly wrong. Your pride is easily dented now.

23 FRIDAY *Moon Age Day 23   Moon Sign Taurus*

You should be making the very best of your leisure time and with the weekend ahead it is clear that travel in particular is on your mind. The way others behave, especially at work, has a strong bearing on your own motivations and ideas. People from the past may make a return to your life on a regular basis around now.

24 SATURDAY *Moon Age Day 24   Moon Sign Gemini*

It looks like you might be at odds with someone today, though it is important to realise that this would be a complete waste of time. The fact is that you are simply not working at your best. To try and push forward under such circumstances would be a mistake so keep your ambitions moderate, if only for the moment.

25 SUNDAY
Moon Age Day 25   Moon Sign Gemini

Though you display high energy levels at work, it could seem as though at least some of your effort is being squandered. This might be due to the presence of people who seem determined to throw obstacles in your path. Concentrate less on this possibility and more on forging your own path no matter what.

26 MONDAY
Moon Age Day 26   Moon Sign Cancer

There are plenty of people you can rely on at present, especially at work. This is a high-profile period on the professional scene and a time you will not wish to squander. The most important fact is that those who have it within their power to influence your life see that you get on well.

27 TUESDAY
Moon Age Day 27   Moon Sign Cancer

You certainly intend to be noticed today but don't overdo things because you may not have the staying power necessary to maintain such a high profile. The lunar high is not too far away and some time spent thinking and planning would certainly not be wasted. Conforming to expectations might be difficult.

28 WEDNESDAY
Moon Age Day 28   Moon Sign Leo

This would be a very good time to make changes, probably in and around your home. However, there are also trends that both encourage and support travel plans. Those Virgoans who have chosen this period to take a holiday are unlikely to be disappointed with what they discover.

29 THURSDAY
Moon Age Day 29   Moon Sign Leo

All you have to do in order to get on well with life is to let your natural light shine. There is a fine line between showing your abilities and appearing pushier than you would wish, however. The greatest gift of Virgo now is its openness. If you remember this fact, you won't go far wrong.

30 FRIDAY
Moon Age Day 0   Moon Sign Virgo

There is great potential around now and you won't want to waste a minute of it. Your opinions are particularly important to others and maintaining a strong presence is much less difficult than it might sometimes seem. Financially speaking you could be on a roll and will want to exploit the situation.

31 SATURDAY
Moon Age Day 1   Moon Sign Virgo

Most of what you take on today could find you on a winning streak and more than anxious to make a good impression on others. Although you might find that not everyone seems to be on your side, it shouldn't be difficult to bring others round to your unique point of view. A little cautious speculation, not necessarily monetary, could turn out well.

September

2019

1 SUNDAY
Moon Age Day 2   Moon Sign Libra

Most of your truly rewarding moments today are likely to come through associations with house and home. People show you how fond they are of you and might be offering to help you in tangible ways. Stay away from controversy at work and stick to your own way of doing things.

2 MONDAY
Moon Age Day 3   Moon Sign Libra

You could be all fingers and thumbs today, which is exactly why you should leave any delicate jobs at least until tomorrow. There are some crucial decisions to be made soon, if not by you then in your vicinity. If your opinions are sought you should prepare yourself to tell the truth as you genuinely see it.

3 TUESDAY
Moon Age Day 4   Moon Sign Scorpio

A deep understanding of specific situations lies at the heart of your efforts today. Don't allow yourself to be bullied into doing anything that goes against the grain and instead allow your conscience to rule your decision-making. A good day for romance and for allowing personal matters to take their course.

4 WEDNESDAY
Moon Age Day 5   Moon Sign Scorpio

Nostalgia might be tugging at your heartstrings on one or two occasions today. Maybe you are looking at some family snaps or meeting someone you haven't seen for quite some time. Whatever the reason, you also need to be aware that life is worth living for now and that there is little future in the past.

5 THURSDAY
Moon Age Day 6   Moon Sign Scorpio

Progress is not fast today in the workplace but should be more noticeable in terms of relationships. Look out for a little money coming your way, possibly as a result of some good luck. Leave some of the more boring jobs for others to do, particularly family members who may not be pulling their weight.

6 FRIDAY
Moon Age Day 7   Moon Sign Sagittarius

There are many things you want to get done today, but whether you get around to tackling them remains to be seen. What would really suit you best might be a change of scene and the chance to look at rolling oceans or high hills. If you are able to be in the company of people you really love, then so much the better.

7 SATURDAY
Moon Age Day 8   Moon Sign Sagittarius

You can be somewhat touchy today and your ego can quite easily be deflated. At the same time, you have a great sense of humour, which could be of great importance when you are dealing with people who seem to be simply born awkward. A slight family dilemma may end up being the cause of much hilarity.

8 SUNDAY
Moon Age Day 9   Moon Sign Capricorn

Your powers of persuasion are quite strong now, leading you into situations that mean getting your own way far more than you might have expected. Even where you do find yourself up against it, the natural good nature displayed by Virgo at its best is easy to see. With a new week ahead, you will want to do some planning now.

9 MONDAY
Moon Age Day 10   Moon Sign Capricorn

A few sharp comments made by you today might not go down all that well with certain other people. You need to be very careful what you say because there are some sensitive types around, and you can be quite prickly. Stay around people you know well because they are less likely to react badly towards you.

10 TUESDAY   *Moon Age Day 11   Moon Sign Aquarius*

Put your personality to the test and make others realise that you are around. This is no time to be hiding your light under a bushel. The best things come to you at present when you are willing to be out there in the limelight. This position is not always comfortable for Virgo, but it works at present.

11 WEDNESDAY   *Moon Age Day 12   Moon Sign Aquarius*

Romantic issues suit you well today and act as a sort of platform for your ego, which is strong at this time. A busy day is in store, so it would be sensible to be out of bed and active early. You should be generally confident, but particularly so when you are doing things you really understand.

12 THURSDAY   *Moon Age Day 13   Moon Sign Aquarius*

It is at this time that doing your own thing seems most important. There are moments today when you simply don't want to follow the instructions of others, especially not people who you feel don't know what they are talking about. It may be necessary to bite your tongue, though you might not be able to avoid a little sarcasm.

13 FRIDAY   *Moon Age Day 14   Moon Sign Pisces*

The lunar low makes it much easier for you to watch life happen, rather than specifically taking part all that much. Nevertheless there is work to be done and even if you don't feel like starting it, you will be better off later. Stay away from people who seem determined to drop you in it or who won't co-operate.

14 SATURDAY   *Moon Age Day 15   Moon Sign Pisces*

Some slight setbacks to everyday progress are indicated, but it would be fair to say that the lunar low does not have the same part to play in your day as appeared to be the case yesterday. Maybe it is because you are keeping busy and probably getting out of the house at some stage. A little shopping might be a good idea.

15 SUNDAY
Moon Age Day 16   Moon Sign Aries

Although you are fairly self-centred right now, it is also possible for you to do others a great deal of good. The fact is that you can think up ways to help most people and also yourself. Sociable and generally kind, you could be called upon to offer a degree of special support to someone who is desperately in need.

16 MONDAY
Moon Age Day 17   Moon Sign Aries

Mundane matters could prove to be somewhat tiresome today and you will want to ring the changes just as much as you can. You will need the company of interesting people if you want to get the most out of the day and should be thinking about those who have an exciting attitude to life.

17 TUESDAY
Moon Age Day 18   Moon Sign Aries

Your ego is on the increase and this might lead to one or two people looking at you sideways. So often you go through life without making a ripple on the water, so when you are up-front it can come as a surprise. Concentrate on specific jobs at work and don't be put off by those with a negative attitude.

18 WEDNESDAY
Moon Age Day 19   Moon Sign Taurus

In a planetary sense, much is now geared towards happy social events and strong romantic experiences, which set the seal on the sort of time you can expect. It shouldn't be hard to settle into the company of those you love, and most of the people around you show you their better and more caring side.

19 THURSDAY
Moon Age Day 20   Moon Sign Taurus

Try to vary your routines as much as you can today because tedium follows if you always do the expected thing. There is a slight tendency for you to retreat into yourself, something that perhaps should be avoided around now. Money matters may seem to strengthen but avoid any extra spending as this could be a state of mind.

20 FRIDAY
Moon Age Day 21   Moon Sign Gemini

There are both major and minor gains staring you in the face today, the question is whether or not you realise it. This is a time to keep your eyes wide open and a period during which you should not allow the restrictive practises and opinions of others to get in your way. Avoid family arguments.

21 SATURDAY
Moon Age Day 22   Moon Sign Gemini

You might be in too much of a rush as Saturday begins. If this turns out to be the case, expect to make a few mistakes. Slow and steady wins the race for you this weekend. Look at potential problems one at a time instead of allowing them to wash over you in waves.

22 SUNDAY
Moon Age Day 23   Moon Sign Gemini

You can have the best of all worlds today, just as long as you remain cool, calm and collected. There are specific difficulties around, probably related to home and family members, but these are only of a fleeting importance. There is something very special on offer romantically but you will need to seek it out.

23 MONDAY
Moon Age Day 24   Moon Sign Cancer

The place where the most progress is likely to be made today is at work. However, the very charitable side of your nature is also on display and this allows you to work hard for the good of others. It may be hard to conform to expectations at home, and you could be surprising some people with your stance.

24 TUESDAY
Moon Age Day 25   Moon Sign Cancer

You want to stay as busy as possible today, though this won't necessarily be possible. Little details keep holding you back and prevent you from making the progress you would wish. Simply keep your mind on the task at hand and keep others at arm's length if they try to confuse or distract you.

25 WEDNESDAY
Moon Age Day 26   Moon Sign Leo

This would be an excellent time to get out and meet others, perhaps in social settings that you particularly enjoy. Sporting activities might also appear to have a strong appeal for Virgo at the moment. Be careful though, because there is a tendency for you to expect too much of yourself too soon.

26 THURSDAY
Moon Age Day 27   Moon Sign Leo

When it comes to impressing others you will probably have little difficulty today. Trends suggest you may be somewhat down in the dumps, probably for no obvious reason. Some Virgoans are likely to retreat into comfort and a strong sense of security, which probably means home.

27 FRIDAY
Moon Age Day 28   Moon Sign Virgo

There isn't much doubt that as September moves towards October, you find yourself in the best position of all to make significant progress. Brave and confident now, you don't mind confronting issues if necessary. Support for your plans should be good, mainly because of your own attitude.

28 SATURDAY
Moon Age Day 0   Moon Sign Virgo

You have a part to play in major decisions right now. Today should reflect a host of positive trends, both professional and social. With the weekend here you could decide to make this evening very special and this is one of those times when you can afford to burn the candle at both ends.

29 SUNDAY
Moon Age Day 1   Moon Sign Libra

It is on the work front that the most inspirational trends now come along. This could be something of a pity if you are a Virgo who doesn't work at the weekend. However, even if you can't do anything concrete today, you can still think and plan ahead. Family members should be attentive and interesting.

30 MONDAY   *Moon Age Day 2   Moon Sign Libra*

You seem to be rather pushy today, probably because you are anxious to get ahead and to use almost any means at your disposal to prove your capabilities. Avoid family disputes and if possible do what you can to prevent them. A change of scene for today would probably do everyone a lot of good.

October 2019

1 TUESDAY
Moon Age Day 3   Moon Sign Scorpio

There are some wonderful surprises in store for Virgo today, but you will have to keep your eye on the ball to gain from any of them. It's possible that not everyone is on your side at work, but those who are not probably have something to gain from opposing you. Don't rise to the bait!

2 WEDNESDAY
Moon Age Day 4   Moon Sign Scorpio

A time of social highlights comes along, with plenty of opportunities to have fun. Present astrological trends make it likely that you are casting your mind forward to the medium-term future, perhaps to Christmas. Longer-term plans might have to be put on hold for a variety of different and generally tedious reasons.

3 THURSDAY
Moon Age Day 5   Moon Sign Sagittarius

You definitely enjoy being busy today and can make the best out of almost any situation. Watch out for the odd minor mishap, probably brought about as a result of carelessness exhibited by someone else. Your present quick thinking makes you good to have around in any tight corner.

4 FRIDAY
Moon Age Day 6   Moon Sign Sagittarius

Romance not only becomes more likely, but more potentially rewarding too. Things that irritated you earlier in the week are now much more likely to make you laugh instead. It might be good to look for a change of scene and an alteration in your routines this Friday. Money matters may begin to look stronger.

5 SATURDAY
Moon Age Day 7   Moon Sign Capricorn

Now is the time to be enjoying good social trends and to be letting people know just how capable you are. Controlling all aspects of your life isn't going to be particularly easy, but you care less about certain issues at this time. Relationships should be working out particularly well and offering new insights.

6 SUNDAY
Moon Age Day 8   Moon Sign Capricorn

Talks with others can find you making some unexpected headway. For many Virgoans, this is a day of rest, but this might not appeal to you under today's trends. As a result, don't be surprised to find yourself out of bed early and anxious to get on with life just as quickly as you are able.

7 MONDAY
Moon Age Day 9   Moon Sign Capricorn

A rather more problematic series of trends come along today, some of which could find you disagreeing with people who normally are no problem. The fault could be yours, so it is important to stand back and look again. As long as you are reasonable, any sort of compromise eventually becomes possible.

8 TUESDAY
Moon Age Day 10   Moon Sign Aquarius

Professional developments should be working out quite well, leaving you with more time to please yourself. If life is plain sailing, take some time out. The year is growing older and there are still some personal goals you have not set out to achieve. A big plan is worth another very careful look now.

9 WEDNESDAY
Moon Age Day 11   Moon Sign Aquarius

It is likely you could talk anyone into doing anything for you now. There are one or two individuals around at this time that you look at with slight mistrust, though probably for no good reason. There won't be time to do everything you would wish today, so it is important to look carefully at priorities.

10 THURSDAY
Moon Age Day 12   Moon Sign Pisces

A three-day lunar low comes along for Virgo. At some times of the year this might be a cause for some concern, but you have been pushing yourself so hard of late that a reduction in pressure ought to be no bad thing. Comfort and security are on your mind now and you might even decide to take a day more or less completely to yourself.

11 FRIDAY
Moon Age Day 13   Moon Sign Pisces

When things get quiet, Virgo spends time pampering itself. Why not? You have put in a great deal of effort so far this month and you deserve to have a decent rest. If, on the other hand, you have to work today, do as little as you can and allow others to fill in where possible. This could be a fairly uneventful day.

12 SATURDAY
Moon Age Day 14   Moon Sign Pisces

You may discover that some people are far less assertive than usual, and you can put that down to your own attitude. It's a fact that you don't brook any interference right now and that those around you realise it. The more you get done today, the greater is the likelihood that you can enjoy a peaceful Saturday.

13 SUNDAY
Moon Age Day 15   Moon Sign Aries

Much of today is geared towards practical matters, though it doesn't have to be that way. Virtually nothing in your life would fall apart if you decided to take some time off. There are people around who would enjoy your company and many responsibilities will run themselves. Enjoy yourself for a while.

14 MONDAY
Moon Age Day 16   Moon Sign Aries

Right now, making up your mind regarding even a crucial personal matter is not going to be at all easy. It might be best to defer decisions until later. By that time you will have had the chance to seek out the advice of someone you trust implicitly. Friends are easy to make and not easily lost at this time.

15 TUESDAY · _Moon Age Day 17 · Moon Sign Taurus_

Emotions could be quite close to the surface now, which is a state of affairs Virgo doesn't like too much. Although you are generally warm, your personal opinions and character tend to be hidden. Feeling as transparent as a sheet of glass is not especially comfortable for anyone born under your zodiac sign.

16 WEDNESDAY · _Moon Age Day 18 · Moon Sign Taurus_

There are times when it is sensible to lend a hand and other occasions when it is much better to simply mind your own business. Although as a general rule you are quite willing to do whatever you can for others, they will not always be particularly pleased to have you around. Some discretion is called for today.

17 THURSDAY · _Moon Age Day 19 · Moon Sign Taurus_

You know when to open your mouth today and those occasions when it would be better to keep your counsel. People you haven't seen for ages come into your life, probably at a very opportune time. There are many things about today that you would class as distinctly odd but the day is still useful.

18 FRIDAY · _Moon Age Day 20 · Moon Sign Gemini_

You have it in mind to treat yourself in some way and the lure of luxury is very strong around now. If you have the chance to travel, you should grab it with both hands, and you can make great gains through the involvement of friends in your life. All in all, this should be a very positive period.

19 SATURDAY · _Moon Age Day 21 · Moon Sign Gemini_

Right now, outdoor activities seem to hold a particular reward for you. Perhaps your sporting side is beginning to show or it could be that you just feel like a walk in the fresh air. Keep up your efforts to move ahead professionally and listen to the wise advice of some very good friends at this time.

20 SUNDAY   *Moon Age Day 22   Moon Sign Cancer*

This is a time when you can get on well in a practical sense. Taking all you have learned in the past, you apply your experience to matters in the practical world and come up with answers that others will think have a hint of genius about them. Don't be too quick to judge the actions of your friends.

21 MONDAY   *Moon Age Day 23   Moon Sign Cancer*

There is slightly less personal ego about today, which is useful when you are mixing with others. Virgo is now a good team player and you should get on well in groups or organisations of any sort. The loner in you takes a back seat at present, leaving you in a good position to join in with new ideas and enterprises.

22 TUESDAY   *Moon Age Day 24   Moon Sign Leo*

You want to have your own way and you decide that you are going to get it now. This is the less attractive face of Virgo as far as other people are concerned and you should at least try to modify the slightly selfish qualities that show at this time. Avoid confusion in personal matters by explaining yourself.

23 WEDNESDAY   *Moon Age Day 25   Moon Sign Leo*

Your instinct to say 'leave it to me' in any situation today is applauded by quite a few people and it is true that you seem to be able to do things on your own that are more difficult in groups. Virgo is very practical and capable, a fact that shows all too clearly. However, you are less likely to go it alone in personal matters.

24 THURSDAY   *Moon Age Day 26   Moon Sign Virgo*

The Moon moves gradually into your zodiac sign today, and brings with it a desire to do as much as you can, as quickly as possible. Despite a wealth of opportunities it would advisable to tackle jobs one at a time. At least that way you can be sure you do all of them to the best of your ability.

25 FRIDAY
Moon Age Day 27   Moon Sign Virgo

The Moon is still on your side, so get cracking and keep busy. With everything to prove, and a vitality that is second to none, it's unlikely that you will be overlooked in anything. Routines are really for the birds at this time and you will want to do whatever takes your fancy, at the time of your choice.

26 SATURDAY
Moon Age Day 28   Moon Sign Libra

Beware of coming on too strong, particularly if you are at the start of a new relationship. You may need to compromise a little in order to accommodate someone else, whilst at the same time showing the real you when it matters most. Confidences come in thick and fast from friends.

27 SUNDAY
Moon Age Day 0   Moon Sign Libra

Seeking out a variety of interests could be fun this Sunday and would certainly be better than sitting around and waiting for life to come to you. Although some jobs might take you longer than you anticipate, the Virgo need to do things properly is in evidence. Friends should be both warm and supportive.

28 MONDAY
Moon Age Day 1   Moon Sign Scorpio

There may be significant improvement in relationships at the beginning of this week. Routines are easy to deal with, though you would rather be having a good time, probably in the company of people you find interesting and stimulating. The everyday world can seem just a little tedious now.

29 TUESDAY
Moon Age Day 2   Moon Sign Scorpio

Plenty of information is coming your way at the moment and it is up to you to use it wisely. Don't turn away advice, even though you will not take notice of it all and be willing to use your charm, which can win you friends. Having an influence on the world is important to you now.

30 WEDNESDAY   *Moon Age Day 3   Moon Sign Sagittarius*

It may now be time to pick up one specific matter than you have let ride for the last two or three days. It could be a worry you have at home, or something practical you know needs to be done. Address such matters today, but remember that there are many fun-filled opportunities as well. Divide your time wisely.

31 THURSDAY   *Moon Age Day 4   Moon Sign Sagittarius*

Some typically Virgoan qualities are on display today, especially your possessive tendency. If you know they are around you can do something about them. Friendships prove to be particularly important and you might force yourself to go that extra mile in order to help someone out of a dilemma.

♍ November 2019

1 FRIDAY
☿ *Moon Age Day 5* *Moon Sign Sagittarius*

The pursuit of wealth might now be on your list of priorities. Virgo may not be the most acquisitive of the zodiac signs, but its thoughts do turn in that direction from time to time, in order to enhance its sense of security. Think ahead and plan some deals that will feather your nest in years to come.

2 SATURDAY
☿ *Moon Age Day 6* *Moon Sign Capricorn*

Stay clear of disagreements today if you can possibly manage to do so. It would be better not to interact too much with people at all rather than to find yourself involved in pointless rows. Such a state of affairs is far less likely in deep attachments. Virgos who are looking for love should have some success now.

3 SUNDAY
☿ *Moon Age Day 7* *Moon Sign Capricorn*

A period during which help is at hand if you need it continues apace, so don't assume you have to do everything for yourself now. On the contrary, people are only too willing to put themselves out on your behalf and will continue to do so for a while. Even those you don't know very well can be especially considerate.

4 MONDAY
☿ *Moon Age Day 8* *Moon Sign Aquarius*

There isn't a great deal of dynamic ambition in Virgo's chart today, but this is only a very short trend, which is due to end almost immediately. For the moment, you will be happy to watch life go by and less inclined than of late to look for riotous social company. Enjoy a little nostalgia now.

5 TUESDAY ☿ *Moon Age Day 9* *Moon Sign Aquarius*

On a practical level, you are quite pressured, but this fact will not prevent you from getting on well all the same. Out here near the middle of the week, and in the midst of some demanding situations, there are people who buckle under the pressure. You, fortunately, are not one of them. Lend support to those who need it.

6 WEDNESDAY ☿ *Moon Age Day 10* *Moon Sign Pisces*

Instead of offering support, you now find yourself receiving it. Potentially speaking, the arrival of the lunar low can take the wind out of your sails, but if you are prepared, the situation will not be half as bad. There are confidences to keep, and although practical matters are on the back burner, love and attention is very noticeable.

7 THURSDAY ☿ *Moon Age Day 11* *Moon Sign Pisces*

Compromise is your middle name today, or at least it if isn't, then it should be. You can get more today by being willing to give a little than at just about any other time this month. Some nostalgia creeps in, but that is part of the way the lunar low makes its presence felt in your life. By tomorrow you will be flying high again.

8 FRIDAY ☿ *Moon Age Day 12* *Moon Sign Pisces*

Whatever is happening today helps you to feel a good deal more secure, never a bad state of affairs for Virgo. Conforming to expectations is what you appear to be doing, though below the surface things are different. The slightly rebellious side of your nature is at work, though like the frantic legs of a swan it is below the surface.

9 SATURDAY ☿ *Moon Age Day 13* *Moon Sign Aries*

Social encounters look good and are inclined to inspire you to try new possibilities. You may get an opportunity to meet people who may be in a good position to offer you advice, and the association you have with others at this time could start your mind thinking along new lines.

10 SUNDAY ☿ *Moon Age Day 14   Moon Sign Aries*

Though you feel generally that you are now less in control of your own life in some ways, as long as you are willing to co-operate with others, this should not really prove to be a particular issue. Get on-side with those who have ideas that broadly parallel your own and don't be afraid to take a few calculated risks.

11 MONDAY ☿ *Moon Age Day 15   Moon Sign Taurus*

Someone might be trying to put you down in the minds of others, or at least that's how it will appear to you right now. It is likely that you are not looking at things quite as logically as would normally be the case and emotions can get in your way. The most important thing is to keep a smile on your face, even when you feel jumpy.

12 TUESDAY ☿ *Moon Age Day 16   Moon Sign Taurus*

This is not a day during which you can afford to take anything for granted. You should check and double-check all details, especially if any of them are related to travel. Staying in one place could prove to be something of a bind, particularly when movement looks so potentially interesting and rewarding.

13 WEDNESDAY ☿ *Moon Age Day 17   Moon Sign Taurus*

Your love life is apt to be a high point today. Single Virgos ought to find a good deal of attention coming their way, whilst those in settled relationships might find a new understanding and contentment. Practical progress could be slightly restricted, but since you are busy in other ways, this won't matter.

14 THURSDAY ☿ *Moon Age Day 18   Moon Sign Gemini*

You can probably expect a good deal of attention coming your way around this time. This will happen in both a personal and in a more general sense. Popularity is everything to you now and you won't hold back in terms of the love you offer in return. Almost anyone can feel your warmth now.

15 FRIDAY ☿ *Moon Age Day 19* *Moon Sign Gemini*

A much more settled period comes along as far as your personal life is concerned. Don't be too quick to offer advice, because you could find yourself refusing the same suggestions yourself before very long. Courage is necessary in public situations, but you should come good in sporting activities.

16 SATURDAY ☿ *Moon Age Day 20* *Moon Sign Cancer*

There may be some hopeful news arriving regarding your personal objectives and wishes. Although not everyone appears to be on your side today, especially at work, you can forge a positive path and impress a few important people on the way. Leave some time free later for romantic moments.

17 SUNDAY ☿ *Moon Age Day 21* *Moon Sign Cancer*

A rather thorny problem could arise today and you may need to be fairly circumspect in the way you choose to deal with it. There is still help around if you want it, though you could be rather insular on occasions and might even think that to ask for assistance is beneath your dignity.

18 MONDAY ☿ *Moon Age Day 22* *Moon Sign Leo*

There could be one or two shortcuts to success for Virgo now, especially if you keep your eyes open. Figures in authority tend to be on your side at the start of this new working week and you should also find friends being especially helpful. Concentrate on a specific matter early in the day and generalise later.

19 TUESDAY ☿ *Moon Age Day 23* *Moon Sign Leo*

Travel could easily be on your mind today. Maybe you have decided that the time is right to visit a relative or a friend who lives at a distance. There is a restless streak present that makes it difficult for you to stay in the same place. Utilising this wanderlust can seem to be very important.

20 WEDNESDAY ☿   *Moon Age Day 24*   *Moon Sign Leo*

Along comes a time that proves to be particularly good for social adventures and for general co-operation. Be willing to compromise and others will relinquish a great deal of the control of situations to you. Virgo may not see itself as a natural leader, but those around you respect both your views and actions.

21 THURSDAY   *Moon Age Day 25*   *Moon Sign Virgo*

Get an early start today and realise, right from the start, that fortune now favours the brave. The lunar high brings you the chance to shine, and should lift your spirits considerably, bearing in mind the way you have been thinking and acting across the last few days. Be prepared to take the odd chance.

22 FRIDAY   *Moon Age Day 26*   *Moon Sign Virgo*

Another potentially good day and a time during which you will be making the most of just about any opportunity that comes your way. Creatively speaking you know what looks and feels right and you can gain support from some unexpected directions. You could surprise yourself with your boldness right now.

23 SATURDAY   *Moon Age Day 27*   *Moon Sign Libra*

You need a sense of movement and space in your life today, which is why you won't take kindly to being held back or restricted in your movements. You have plenty of energy and that might make this a rip-roaring sort of weekend. However, deep inside, you could be quaking at the thought of some of the things you are doing.

24 SUNDAY   *Moon Age Day 28*   *Moon Sign Libra*

Handling several different tasks at the same time is not at all difficult right now but you do need to be just a little careful that you don't tire yourself too much. This is Sunday after all and is supposed to be a time when you get some rest. Confusion over personal and family matters should soon be dealt with.

25 MONDAY   *Moon Age Day 29   Moon Sign Scorpio*

You are good company to have around today, which is why it feels as though your popularity is going off the scale. Keeping up with all the invitations that come along could be difficult and so it may be necessary to let someone down. Prepare for a busy phase with new opportunities arriving all the time.

26 TUESDAY   *Moon Age Day 0   Moon Sign Scorpio*

Your desire to make important changes to your life might be somewhat smothered by the attitude and actions of family members or friends at the moment. As a result, some patience is necessary, a fact that also seems to be true at work. Fortunately you come from a zodiac sign that has a lot of patience at the moment.

27 WEDNESDAY   *Moon Age Day 1   Moon Sign Sagittarius*

You may now either have to make significant changes to a recent project or perhaps scrap it altogether. Some fresh air would probably do you good today and you certainly won't take kindly to being trapped in the same place all day. New social possibilities offer change and diversity later on.

28 THURSDAY   *Moon Age Day 2   Moon Sign Sagittarius*

It could be that you find yourself at odds with others close to the end of November and you will need to think up new strategies to get them on your side. If your opinions are being ignored, there really isn't much point in losing your temper over it. By tomorrow you should find those around you more understanding.

29 FRIDAY   *Moon Age Day 3   Moon Sign Capricorn*

Though getting on with others is not difficult today, you could find them to be rather less decisive than you would wish. Don't try to please too many people because it simply won't work. It might be necessary to let those you love make their own mistakes since it is probably the only way they will learn valuable lessons.

30 SATURDAY   *Moon Age Day 4   Moon Sign Capricorn*

There is a great thirst for adventure in today's chart for Virgo and a determination that is stronger than you have registered for a month or two. Get as much done as you can today because you have boundless energy and your sense of purpose is second to none. Family arrangements might have to be deferred to accommodate your state of mind.

December

2019

1 SUNDAY
Moon Age Day 5   Moon Sign Aquarius

You are well aware what elements of your life deserve your attention today – even though one or two people might think that they know different. Spend time with family members and do what you can to support a friend who could well be going through a rough phase right now.

2 MONDAY
Moon Age Day 6   Moon Sign Aquarius

Compromises in relationships are a natural part of what you will encounter at the present time. If you refuse to make them, problems could come along later. Stay away from conflict in your family, or amongst friends. The problem is not one of failing to hold your own, but rather being too aggressive.

3 TUESDAY
Moon Age Day 7   Moon Sign Aquarius

Some of your efforts to keep life under control may be going wrong. The results are likely to be more amusing than annoying, though there could be times today when the odd frustration will creep in. Once again, it is important to avoid confrontation with people who are not really worth your effort.

4 WEDNESDAY
Moon Age Day 8   Moon Sign Pisces

Get ready for a couple of days during which it will be difficult to get everything you want from life. The lunar low is holding you back, but not all that much. As long as you stick to planning, and leave a few of the more concrete jobs until the back end of the week, you will hardly be held up at all this month.

5 THURSDAY
Moon Age Day 9   Moon Sign Pisces

Stick to the simple things of life and spend some time spoiling yourself. There is an active and very demanding period ahead, so it won't do you any harm to charge up those batteries. Your confidence should not be dented unless you come face to face with people who seem determined to put you down.

6 FRIDAY
Moon Age Day 10   Moon Sign Aries

Planetary trends suggest that there is little in the way of harmony in your relationships today, and part of the reason for this could be frustrations on your part that you find difficult to address. Talk to people and truly listen to what they have to say. Compromise is necessary and could help you through this time.

7 SATURDAY
Moon Age Day 11   Moon Sign Aries

The emotional rewards from intimate relationships are showing much more clearly now. Your confidence rises as you realise that people are really listening to what you have to say. Take situations by the scruff of the neck and be willing to grab the odd chance, which under normal circumstances you may shy away from.

8 SUNDAY
Moon Age Day 12   Moon Sign Aries

It's time for a short break from obligations. Maybe you have some time off work, or at least are relinquishing a few of the responsibilities that you would normally take on. For whatever reason, you have the chance for a steadier day, and will probably grab it with both hands.

9 MONDAY
Moon Age Day 13   Moon Sign Taurus

You may be anxious to get on with plans for the future, but there are some restrictions around at present that will hold you up somewhat. Family concerns that are somehow related to plans for Christmas are not likely to delay you for long because you are able to think up new strategies on the hoof.

10 TUESDAY   *Moon Age Day 14   Moon Sign Taurus*

You may need a little mental refreshment at any time now. That means ringing the changes and mixing with people who are not normally part of your circle. It may dawn on you today that Christmas is quite close, leaving you less time than you thought to get everything done the way you would wish.

11 WEDNESDAY   *Moon Age Day 15   Moon Sign Gemini*

Get ready to make tracks and get ahead professionally. With one eye on the season and the other on what you want to achieve materially, there isn't a great deal of time to spare right now. Don't overbook yourself for the forthcoming weekend. It's getting close to Christmas and there may be shopping you have forgotten.

12 THURSDAY   *Moon Age Day 16   Moon Sign Gemini*

You appear to be taking the initiative more than usual today and that gets you noticed. You can now get a great deal done, even if your attitude towards some situations is rather unusual. Don't rush your fences because there is plenty of time to get jobs sorted properly, even if you start to feel it is running out.

13 FRIDAY   *Moon Age Day 17   Moon Sign Cancer*

Social matters may not be quite as rewarding today as you had probably hoped, mainly because of the attitude of others, which is not what you had come to expect. Although there is plenty to keep you occupied all day, you will need some space to simply sit and think; an essential for Virgo now and again.

14 SATURDAY   *Moon Age Day 18   Moon Sign Cancer*

Give and take is in short supply, especially from your loved ones. Although you consider yourself to be particularly giving at present, the same attitude doesn't appear to be coming back in your direction. Maybe you are concentrating on the wrong people and should be looking towards friends, rather than relatives?

15 SUNDAY   *Moon Age Day 19   Moon Sign Cancer*

You are especially impressionable and very sensitive this Sunday, a fact that won't be lost on the people you mix with for most of the time. Although the day can be quite busy, there are moments during which you can stop and think. Rushing around might spoil much of what today is about.

16 MONDAY   *Moon Age Day 20   Moon Sign Leo*

The romantic view of life is fine, but it won't do very much for you today. Now is a time to be hard-nosed and very practical. You are not letting others down as long as you bear their future in mind too, which is clearly what you are doing. All the same, there might be some temporary recriminations.

17 TUESDAY   *Moon Age Day 21   Moon Sign Leo*

You should be able to get the best from communications today and can gain from simply speaking your mind. Not everyone will agree with what you are saying, but most people will at least give you the right to speak out. What matters the most is that you get yourself well and truly noticed.

18 WEDNESDAY   *Moon Age Day 22   Moon Sign Virgo*

This is when you reach your mental and physical peak, just in time for the last run-up to Christmas. It doesn't matter what you take on today, you have the energy and determination to see it through properly. Gains can be made as a result of meetings and discussions that might have taken place some time ago.

19 THURSDAY   *Moon Age Day 23   Moon Sign Virgo*

It might be that something in your life needs to change, even if you can't put your finger on exactly what that might be. Whatever you plan to do today, you should get on with it as soon as you can. Deal with necessities one at a time and don't crowd your schedule, especially with petty worries.

20 FRIDAY
Moon Age Day 24   Moon Sign Libra

You really do want to keep a high profile at the moment and since there is no lack of things to be done, you shouldn't have too much trouble. Someone in your immediate circle shows their kind side, which could take the wind out of your sails a little. Commitments shouldn't get you down at this time.

21 SATURDAY
Moon Age Day 25   Moon Sign Libra

It is not out of the question that you will enjoy arguments today, specifically for the sake of them. Whether this is a good thing or not remains to be seen. There are two levels of disagreement. If you choose the one that leads to a sharpening of your intellect and over which you don't bear any sort of grudge, then there is no problem.

22 SUNDAY
Moon Age Day 26   Moon Sign Scorpio

You now need to be very careful about speaking out of turn. The problem is that you don't have quite the planetary support you might wish all of a sudden and could quite easily put your foot in it. This shouldn't be a problem because Virgo is quite capable of keeping its own counsel.

23 MONDAY
Moon Age Day 27   Moon Sign Scorpio

The pace of developments in your life generally is not going to be great today and you might be rather too outspoken for you own good. However, things do look good on the romantic front and you have what it takes to get others to take notice of you. It is better they see your slightly fractious side than not see you at all.

24 TUESDAY
Moon Age Day 28   Moon Sign Sagittarius

This is still very much a go-ahead period and offers you the vitality to get everything right as the holidays begin. You ought to be in fine spirits and more than willing to have a go at more or less anything. Stay away from contentious topics in conversation now because you are apt to speak your mind when you shouldn't.

25 WEDNESDAY *Moon Age Day 29 Moon Sign Sagittarius*

A great mix of planetary trends surrounds you during Christmas Day. Some of them are quiet, so you may not choose to be socially active all the time. You also receive significant emotional support and return it in kind. Not surprisingly, family associations are well accented right now and should bring contentment.

26 THURSDAY *Moon Age Day 0 Moon Sign Capricorn*

Anything that contributes to a sense of variety is what you are looking for today. You could easily become bored and need to feel that life is stimulating. Taxing your brain is no problem and is something you try to do deliberately. Spend some time with your partner and make sure you whisper the right words at the most appropriate time.

27 FRIDAY *Moon Age Day 1 Moon Sign Capricorn*

Everything is likely to come together at the same time in order to offer you a really enjoyable time right now. You have great certainty, together with obvious warmth, which can be a formidable combination. Since energy levels are high you will not flag, no matter how long the celebrations continue.

28 SATURDAY *Moon Age Day 2 Moon Sign Capricorn*

Perhaps it is now time for a change of scene? You won't get too far today sitting around with your feet up and neither should you be indulging in too much food or drink. Once again, the practical qualities inherent in your zodiac sign show themselves, making it necessary to remain active.

29 SUNDAY *Moon Age Day 3 Moon Sign Aquarius*

It would be a good idea to vary your routines as much as possible today. Variety genuinely is the spice of life as far as you are concerned and in any case, to move around a little prevents you from becoming bored. This is a day that could even turn out to be weird and wonderful in some way.

30 MONDAY
Moon Age Day 4   Moon Sign Aquarius

Matters connected with travel potentially bring a few interesting moments and might lead you to plan a journey that is some time in the future but which will be very important to you. If there are quite a few mundane chores to be undertaken, you won't take kindly to being reminded of them by others.

31 TUESDAY
Moon Age Day 5   Moon Sign Pisces

It appears that this is a particularly good time for any sort of intimacy between yourself and your partner. For those who are not attached, it might be that a friendship takes on a different sort of meaning in your life. Resolutions made today are likely to be as a result of a great deal of thought earlier in the year.

RISING SIGNS FOR VIRGO

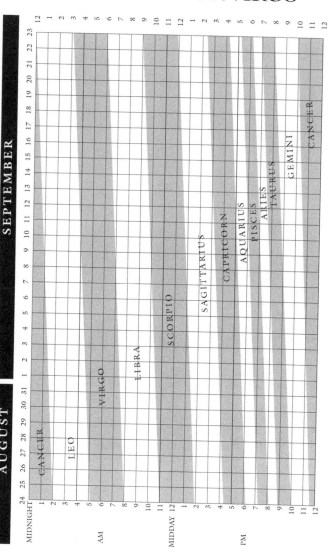

THE ZODIAC, PLANETS
AND CORRESPONDENCES

The Earth revolves around the Sun once every calendar year, so when viewed from Earth the Sun appears in a different part of the sky as the year progresses. In astrology, these parts of the sky are divided into the signs of the zodiac and this means that the signs are organised in a circle. The circle begins with the sign for Aries and ends with Pisces.

Taking the zodiac sign as a starting point, astrologers then work with all the positions of planets, stars and many other factors to calculate horoscopes and birth charts and tell us what the stars have in store for us.

The table below shows the planets and Elements for each of the signs of the zodiac. Each sign belongs to one of the four Elements: Fire, Air, Earth or Water. Fire signs are creative and enthusiastic; Air signs are mentally active and thoughtful; Earth signs are constructive and practical; Water signs are emotional and have strong feelings.

It also shows the metals and gemstones associated with, or corresponding with, each sign. The correspondence is made when a metal or stone possesses properties that are held in common with a particular sign of the zodiac.

Finally, the table shows the opposite of each star sign – this is the opposite sign in the astrological circle.

Placed	Sign	Symbol	Element	Planet	Metal	Stone	Opposite
1	Aries	Ram	Fire	Mars	Iron	Bloodstone	Libra
2	Taurus	Bull	Earth	Venus	Copper	Sapphire	Scorpio
3	Gemini	Twins	Air	Mercury	Mercury	Tiger's Eye	Sagittarius
4	Cancer	Crab	Water	Moon	Silver	Pearl	Capricorn
5	Leo	Lion	Fire	Sun	Gold	Ruby	Aquarius
6	Virgo	Maiden	Earth	Mercury	Mercury	Sardonyx	Pisces
7	Libra	Scales	Air	Venus	Copper	Sapphire	Aries
8	Scorpio	Scorpion	Water	Pluto	Plutonium	Jasper	Taurus
9	Sagittarius	Archer	Fire	Jupiter	Tin	Topaz	Gemini
10	Capricorn	Goat	Earth	Saturn	Lead	Black Onyx	Cancer
11	Aquarius	Waterbearer	Air	Uranus	Uranium	Amethyst	Leo
12	Pisces	Fishes	Water	Neptune	Tin	Moonstone	Virgo